THE COMPLETE GUIDE TO WING SHOOTING

THE COMPLETE GUIDE TO WING SHOOTING

THE ULTIMATE HANDBOOK TO A SPECIALIZED SPORT

ALEX BRANT

The Lyons Press
Guilford, Connecticut
An imprint of The Globe Pequot Press

To buy books in quantity for corporate use
or incentives, call **(800) 962–0973, ext. 4551,**
or e-mail **premiums@GlobePequot.com.**

The Lyons Press is an imprint of The Globe Pequot Press.

Printed in the United States of America

10 9 8 7 6 5 4 3 2 1

Library of Congress Cataloging-in-Publication Data
Brant, Alex.
The complete guide to wing shooting : the ultimate handbook to a specialized sport / Alex Brant.
    p. cm.
Includes bibliographical references and index.
ISBN 1–59228–648–8 (trade cloth)
    1. Shooting—Handbooks, manuals, etc. I. Title.
SK37.B69 2005
799.2'4—dc22
2005010671

To Renata Coleman, my partner in life and in our shoots. Without her support I never would have written this—so blame her!

To Jose Pepe Fanjul, one of the finest game shots I know. His mischievous sense of humor is, or should be, legendary. He is also a host extraordinaire.

And to the dogs, who shared my life and passion for hunting: English setters—Mr. Zev, Sequoia Sue, Buck, Rose, and CH Cowboys Footsteps; Labradors—Dusty, Darky, Maggie, Sam, Mamba, and Bubba.

CONTENTS

FOREWORD
BY WILL HETHERINGTON

Alex Brant is an American who loves shooting in the U.K. —
well, actually he loves shooting everywhere. However, the
U.K. is one of his favorite hunting grounds, and as his editor at
The Shooting Gazette here in England I have been able to enjoy
his musings on all things shooting for the best part of two years
now. And if there is one thing that has struck me more than anything else in all my dealings with him, it is his unquenchable
love of the sport and interest in every aspect associated with it.

There can't be many people who are able to write authorita-
tively on such diverse subjects as duck hunting on Long Island,
high pheasants in Devon, skeet shooting almost anywhere, and
partridge shooting in Spain. In truth, I am a little jealous of his
shooting experience. Reading stories of great shooting trips
around the globe while sitting at a desk on a rainy day in England
tends to do that to a man. But for you, the reader, it is this experience that gives him the knowledge to make this book both enter-
taining and informative.

From his days in Le Club de la Roue de Roy while at University in Montreal to his time as co-owner of the shooting at
Humewood Castle in Ireland, life has always been about shooting for Alex. He has developed a clear understanding of what
equipment, training, and knowledge are needed to both enjoy a
day in the field and be a successful shot. There is no substitute for
experience when writing about anything, and in this case it is

extensive shooting over many years that allows the author to write so easily about the sport.

As a columnist for *The Shooting Gazette,* Alex has tapped into his diverse experience to produce thought-provoking and informative copy on as wide a range of topics as anyone else who has written for the magazine. And I am glad to report that he has done the same with this book. If his opinions are sometimes strongly held, his writing is all the better for it.

It's a pleasure to be his editor and I'm sure it will be a pleasure for you to read his book.

Will Hetherington
Editor, *The Shooting Gazette*

FOREWORD
BY THOMAS MCINTYRE

Hope, it is said, is the thing with feathers. You can only imagine the sort of hope felt for scores of millennia by men who had devised highly cunning ways of bringing down the largest mammals on earth, only to look into the sky and see feathered creatures of which even the smallest were adept at gracefully eluding capture.

The best that humans might have done would have been to catch birds, on the ground or in the air, in nets—as still takes place today in parts of Europe—or resort to pilfering the eggs from their nests. These were hardly ennobling forms of the chase, especially when compared to those rare occurrences when a flushed bird at the start of its rise might be dropped by a hurled stone or a flung stick, leaving the thrower stunned with surprise, and with an inchoate ambition to do it all over again.

Such moments probably offered only a brief respite from the envy humans must have had for these animals that could travel about freely on the wing. It was an envy that would lead to the sincerest form of imitation in the fabrication of the first "force at a distance" weapon. It was by a man's thinking about the bird, as José Ortega y Gasset reasons in *Meditations on Hunting*, that he "put a beak on one end of a stick and feathers on the other; that is, he created the artificial bird, the arrow, which flies swiftly through the air" toward fleeing animals.

While the arrow and the bow may have made shooting birds marginally more feasible, it was a chain of subsequent developments—gunpowder, the gun, the lock, spherical shot, and not incidentally the percussion cap—that allowed wing shooting, which had begun to be codified during the Restoration in the late 1600s, to enter into complete existence.

With these inventions marking its dateline—and with such continuing improvements as cartridges, chokes, smokeless powders, nontoxic shot, and more—wing shooting has become arguably the most modern of the hunting and firearms sports. Without question it is the most varied and sophisticated.

What qualifies as wing shooting, first of all? Is it passing doves or quail hunted over dogs? Ducks maple-leafing into decoys or tall pheasants driven by beaters? Woodcock? Partridge? The answer, of course, is that it is all of the above, and everything else. It would take a very long time to catalog the totality of the gamebirds of the world, not to mention the assorted types of clay-target games that are also an integral part of wing shooting. And each kind of wing shooting, whether for birds or targets, possesses its own particular nuances of etiquette and tradition, of which the gunner strives to acquire a command as earnestly as he does the techniques of shooting itself.

Gaining a command of the basics of wing shooting—a true command, not merely a certain competence—is the task of a lifetime, something new being learned every time a gun is shouldered. With the almost limitless variations in the types of wing shooting, one man would require an inexhaustible store of lifetimes to come close to a familiarity with them all. For which reason, if someone were to say that he had grown weary of wing shooting, the natural question would be, "How on earth could he possibly know?"

The other timeless quality of wing shooting is the art residing in it. Rifle shooting is an essentially mechanical skill, albeit a refined one. Wing shooting is a skill, too; but there comes a point in it where pure skill must blend with art.

Perhaps the most elemental example of art in wing shooting is lead, or as Alex Brant calls it, "forward allowance." Clearly there is no single prescriptible method for accomplishing it when at least four distinct effective ones can be demonstrated. With a range of choices such as that—not to mention choices of shotgun actions, barrel configurations, gauges, chokes, cartridge lengths, powder loads, shot sizes, ad infinitum—then what you are practicing is most definitely an art, and not merely a skill.

In wing shooting, art finds embodiment even in the sport's fundamental implement, the shotgun. Shotguns are not the first tools, devices, or weapons to be viewed as *objets d'art*; but they are certainly among the very few whose functional form, unembellished, displays artistic elegance. A shotgun that shoots well is one that almost invariably looks good. And in the gun there arises the unique opportunity for the maker of a usable product to imbue it—through engraving, bluing, stock shaping, checkering—with his own aesthetic, rather than strictly utilitarian, vision.

There is more than that to say about wing shooting, and I should let Alex Brant say it. As a final request, though, let us venture that wing shooting is perhaps the most fanciful of the shooting sports, born out of our ancient fascination with the things with feathers. When it comes to all the uses to which we put guns, wing shooting may ultimately be the one in which our fancies are given their most untethered flight. I hope I'm right about that.

Thomas McIntyre
July 2005

Thomas McIntyre has been a regular contributor to Sports Afield *magazine for over twenty-five years, and has written for numerous other publications during that time as well. He is the author of five books, his latest being* Seasons & Days: A Hunting Life, *published by The Lyons Press. He is also the editor of the upcoming anthology* Wild and Fair: Tales of Hunting Big Game in North America.

ACKNOWLEDGMENTS

I'd like to thank everyone at Beretta, especially Peter Horn, my dear old friend who runs their high-end gun division, with whom I've hunted from New York State to the Sudan, and Cathy Williams, who is in charge of public relations. And also Ed Anderson, the gunsmith at Beretta Gallery in New York City, and Robert Booz, the store manager, and Dr. Franco Beretta, who has shown me so many kindnesses.

Thanks also to Richard Purdey, chairman of that venerable firm, who has provided much support and friendship. And to Tom Roster, who shared his huge knowledge of ballistics.

I'm grateful to the great old PR guys who helped me in the beginning, twenty-five years ago: Johnny Falk of Winchester/Olin, Mike Bussard of Federal, and Dick Dietz of Remington. And to the late, great John Amber and John Jobson for their counsel when I was thrown in the deep end editing magazines.

Thanks to editors from the old days to the new: Jay Cassell, Tom Paugh, and Diana Rupp from *Sports Afield*; Mike Barnes and Will Hetherington from *The Shooting Gazette*; Ralph Stuart, Vic Venters, and Silvio Calabi from *Shooting Sportsman*; and John Culler, Chuck Wechsler, and Art Carter from *Sporting Classics*.

Thanks also to Jason Nash of Federal and Eddie Stevenson of Remington for cartridges for testing and photographic support; Cliff Moller and Chuck Webb at Briley for technical assistance; Gary Herman, who influenced my shooting so much; and Robert

Castelli, who has shot so many clays with me and even laughed at my jokes—a true friend.

Finally, thanks to Suzan Bruner, my old friend, who helped with the photography and the patterning for this book.

INTRODUCTION

L ife is funny. Born in America fifty-seven years ago, shooting in Europe for most of forty years, and living in the British Isles for nearly a decade, I have never quite fit in. In the articles I write for *Shooting Sportsman* magazine I'm often accused of being too elitist, while in my articles for the British magazine *The Shooting Gazette*, where I write a monthly shooting column, I'm accused of being too American. Personally, I like to think that I've learned a lot from both the British and American schools of thought and have synthesized a cogent "best of both worlds" school of shooting.

While this book is written primarily for American shooters, I have drawn heavily from my experiences shooting in Europe, South America, and, to a lesser extent, Africa, as well as the United States. I've participated in virtually every kind of shotgun sport, but over the years I've gravitated to driven shooting, as I feel this sport offers the most challenging shooting available. This has allowed me to shoot literally thousands and thousands of shells each year. After all, on a big driven day it's possible to shoot as many birds as a ruffed grouse or woodcock hunter is likely to see in an entire season. Over the course of a shooting season I have the opportunity to experiment with a wide variety of loads and see the results quickly.

Much of what I've learned from shooting tall driven pheasant applies very well to waterfowl shooting and pheasant hunting in the Midwest. And driven partridge has been a wonderful testing ground, one that translates well for shots on quail, dove, woodcock, and teal. The basic mechanics of shooting—stance, gun mount, various methods for establishing lead, shot angles, chokes, patterning, and so on—are relevant and similar for most aspects of shooting sports from walking up wild birds to clay games to driven shoots.

With a title like *The Complete Guide to Wing Shooting*, you would expect this book to cover all the major aspects of shotgunning. And it does, although some of the terminology used might be difficult for someone who knows absolutely nothing about shotguns and shotgun sports to follow. Part of the problem, even though I teach a hundred or so beginners to shoot clays every year,

Camaraderie and good fellowship are integral parts of wing shooting. Pepe Fanjul and I are about to head out quail shooting.

is that it has been four decades since I was a beginner. When talking or writing about shooting, it's difficult for me not to assume that the listener or reader has at least a basic understanding of the sport I love so much. Rest assured, however, that the combined text, photographs, and illustrations will help anyone who reads this book understand the critical elements of proper shooting, along with a multitude of other facets related to the sport.

There is a distinct difference between a "shooter" and a "sportsman." To get the most out of shotgunning, you must become environmentally aware. Start by learning a little bit about the gamebirds you are chasing. Observe the way different birds fly. Even after all these years I'm always amazed at the distances wood pigeons can cover so rapidly, and how when they pause, as if to catch their breath, they drop quickly. By observing pheasants from many angles, I believe I've gained a better feel for their flight tendencies, which has made me a better game shot.

The term "conservationist" was coined by Gifford Pinchot, Secretary of the Interior under Teddy Roosevelt. We who love the outdoors must embrace it and not leave it to the domain of the ill-informed protectionist. It is our responsibility to pick up not only our spent shotshells and soda cans, but also any trash we see that is not quickly biodegradable. By doing something as simple as putting out wooden boxes for wood ducks or a bit of feed in the off-season, you can have a positive impact on the environment.

By the way, there are a few references to English pellet sizes in the following pages due to my years of shooting in the U.K. It's helpful to keep in mind that American pellets and English pellets typically differ somewhat in size. For example, No. 5 shot in the U.K. usually equals No. 6 shot in the U.S.; No. 7 U.K. equals No. 7½ U.S.; and No. 9 shot is basically the same. I have also included the English nomenclature for choke in certain spots (e.g., improved cylinder equates to quarter choke), although everything is discussed in American terms. This applies to loads too, which are always expressed in ounces, with the rough equivalent in grams shown occasionally (e.g., 1¼ ounces equates to around 36 grams).

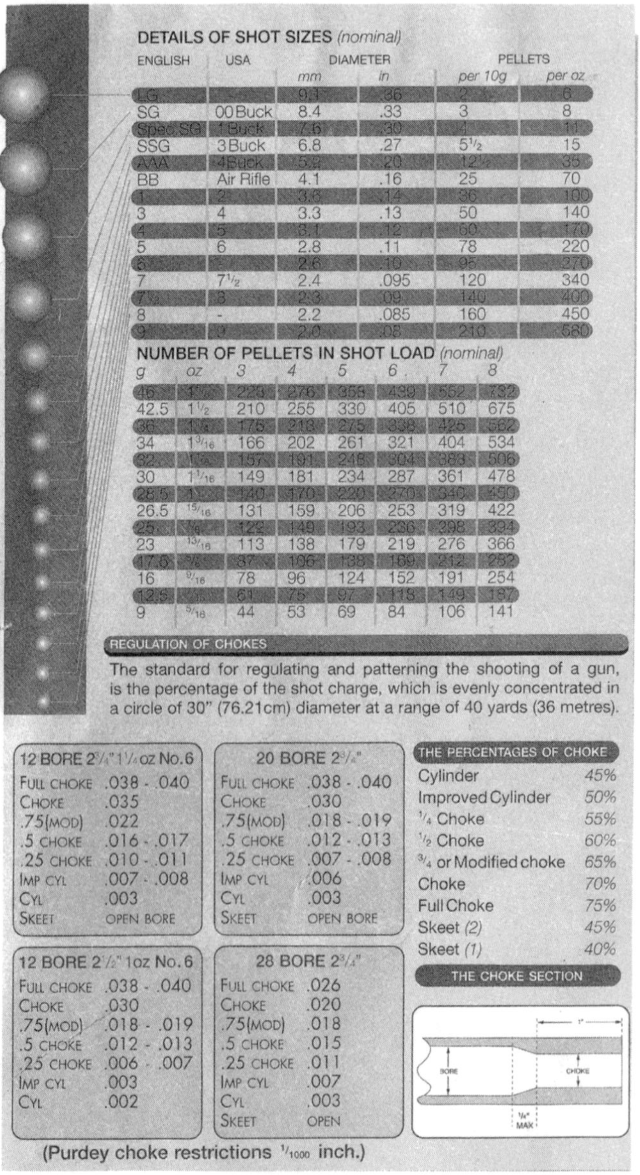

DETAILS OF SHOT SIZES *(nominal)*

ENGLISH	USA	DIAMETER mm	DIAMETER in	PELLETS per 10g	PELLETS per oz
LG		9.1	.36	2	6
SG	00 Buck	8.4	.33	3	8
Spec SG	1 Buck	7.6	.30	4	11
SSG	3 Buck	6.8	.27	5½	15
AAA	4 Buck	5.2	.20	12½	35
BB	Air Rifle	4.1	.16	25	70
1	2	3.6	.14	36	100
3	4	3.3	.13	50	140
4	5	3.1	.12	60	170
5	6	2.8	.11	78	220
6	-	2.6	.10	95	270
7	7½	2.4	.095	120	340
7½	8	2.3	.09	140	400
8	-	2.2	.085	160	450
9	9	2.0	.08	210	580

NUMBER OF PELLETS IN SHOT LOAD *(nominal)*

g	oz	3	4	5	6	7	8
46	1⅝	223	276	358	439	552	732
42.5	1½	210	255	330	405	510	675
36	1¼	175	213	275	338	425	562
34	1 3/16	166	202	261	321	404	534
32	1⅛	157	191	248	304	383	506
30	1 1/16	149	181	234	287	361	478
28.5	1	140	170	220	270	340	450
26.5	15/16	131	159	206	253	319	422
25	⅞	122	149	193	236	298	394
23	13/16	113	138	179	219	276	366
17.5	⅝	87	106	138	169	212	282
16	9/16	78	96	124	152	191	254
12.5	7/16	61	75	97	118	149	187
9	5/16	44	53	69	84	106	141

REGULATION OF CHOKES

The standard for regulating and patterning the shooting of a gun, is the percentage of the shot charge, which is evenly concentrated in a circle of 30" (76.21cm) diameter at a range of 40 yards (36 metres).

12 BORE 2¾" 1¼oz No.6	
FULL CHOKE	.038 - .040
CHOKE	.035
.75(MOD)	.022
.5 CHOKE	.016 - .017
.25 CHOKE	.010 - .011
IMP CYL	.007 - .008
CYL	.003
SKEET	OPEN BORE

20 BORE 2¾"	
FULL CHOKE	.038 - .040
CHOKE	.030
.75(MOD)	.018 - .019
.5 CHOKE	.012 - .013
.25 CHOKE	.007 - .008
IMP CYL	.006
CYL	.003
SKEET	OPEN BORE

12 BORE 2½" 1oz No.6	
FULL CHOKE	.038 - .040
CHOKE	.030
.75(MOD)	.018 - .019
.5 CHOKE	.012 - .013
.25 CHOKE	.006 - .007
IMP CYL	.003
CYL	.002

28 BORE 2¾"	
FULL CHOKE	.026
CHOKE	.020
.75(MOD)	.018
.5 CHOKE	.015
.25 CHOKE	.011
IMP CYL	.007
CYL	.003
SKEET	OPEN

THE PERCENTAGES OF CHOKE	
Cylinder	45%
Improved Cylinder	50%
¼ Choke	55%
½ Choke	60%
¾ or Modified choke	65%
Choke	70%
Full Choke	75%
Skeet *(2)*	45%
Skeet *(1)*	40%

THE CHOKE SECTION

(Purdey choke restrictions 1/1000 inch.)

Courtesy of Purdey

Chapter
1

SHOOTING IN THE UPLANDS

Many of my happiest days have been spent afield with gun and bird dog. For me, no season provides the anticipation of boundless joy as much as autumn. Bright fall colors drape the covers from New York to Montreal, my old stomping grounds. And as the colors fade and the snows fall, stark gray days and leafless trees often provide perfect conditions for grouse shooting. English setters, side-by-side shotguns, and a good pair of boots are just about all I need for a great day in the woods. (Actually I'm not such a minimalist, but these are the core elements.)

While I have on rare occasions been described as a wing-shooting expert, I feel this is more justified in regard to driven shooting than any other aspect of our sport. Nevertheless, I have spent over a thousand days in the uplands in various places around the world. I have shot francolin over pointers in South Africa and perdiz in Argentina, but there are still areas where I've yet to hunt. For example, I haven't walked the plains of Canada in search of sharptails and Hungarian partridge, nor have I climbed the steep cliffs of the Snake River Canyon for chukars.

My teenage days were fairly mundane, yet highly pleasurable. The majority of my shooting time was spent near Pawling,

New York, at Joe Cox's preserve, and to a lesser extent at Suffolk Lodge on Long Island. (This property, along with two or three private clubs in the region, was confiscated under eminent domain and turned into a public park, primarily for the fishing.) Both establishments provided a quality preserve experience, though not of the same standard as offered in the wild. Still, I would occasionally hunt grouse and woodcock at Cox's.

I went to college in Montreal at McGill University. One of the first things I did after signing up for classes was join Le Club de la Roue de Roy. It was one of the better moves of my life. The club was less than an hour south of town. In addition to tower shoots, duck releases, and preserve pheasant, it also provided good woodcock shooting. I became quite friendly with Ricky Longtin, the founder and manager of the club, and a truly great fellow. When he was short of guides, he would occasionally ask me to take one of his German pointers and other members out shooting. I really enjoyed this.

Just before heading to college, I had purchased an English setter from a famous grouse field dog kennel in western Pennsylvania. Mr. Zev was perhaps the smartest dog I've ever owned. He was royally bred, with the blood of dogs like Tennessee Zev, Mississippi Zev, and Sam L's Rebel flowing through his veins. Unfortunately, he was misrouted on the plane trip and spent over a day in transit. After that experience he was always very uncomfortable in cars and prone to carsickness. He became a fair hunter, but nothing more. Still, we were great friends and I miss him even now.

As I grew older, my experience broadened. I shot quail once in the late 1960s north of Palm Beach at Bonette's preserve. While I believe it has improved significantly since then, the shooting, while beautifully laid out with specially designed jeeps and the whole nine yards, was pathetic. These were the worst sort of pen-reared quail. They were so weak that they hardly flew ten yards before settling.

In the early eighties, at Burnt Pines Plantation near Atlanta, I discovered that quail were definitely a bird worth shooting. Here the birds flew well, and there were enough wild birds about to keep things interesting.

In the mid-eighties, I was attending a Racquet Club shoot at Mashomack near Pine Plains, New York. I was walking around with fellow R&T member Edward Ulmann when I met Downs Mallory and his wife, Barbara. The back of their four-wheel drive was packed with good-looking English setters. Through our conversation, I learned Downs was the nephew of Bob Habgood, who had one of the great English setter kennels for grouse trials. He had recently passed away and Downs was slated to inherit his last great dog.

"I don't care how good he is supposed to be, I'm just not taking another dog into the house," stated Barbara.

"I'll buy him," I said, thereby changing my life.

Canadian Open Shooting Dog Champion Cowboys Footsteps worked well for me quail shooting in Alabama.

Delmar Smith styles up Buck in Oklahoma.

Orchard Valley Focus (Ruff) had been trained by Rich Tuttle, who had won the Grand National more than once. Ruff became "Buck" on arrival.

Tuttle told me that Buck was perhaps the best dog that Habgood ever owned. The only reason that he hadn't won grouse trials, and indeed had never been run in them, was because he did not have a high tail carriage. On a good day, it was only about 45 degrees on point. He was, however, brilliant at finding and holding grouse. He was hugely intense. Tuttle told me that he should have been run in champion stakes, because in a year when there weren't many grouse around, that dog could take the trial simply by finding birds. The owner didn't see it that way and just kept him as a personal grouse dog.

I called Johnny Falk, who in addition to being the public relations man for Winchester was also a fine gun dog writer. I asked Johnny for the best method of housebreaking an older dog. He suggested that I kennel him overnight or when I wasn't around; walking him first thing in the morning, twenty minutes after meals, and so on. Buck was housebroken in two days.

That dog was an amazing bird finder.

I often took him with me up to Millbrook to shoot at a friend's farm. He was not a close-working, pussyfooting sort of dog. He ran a big race and would swoop in on a bird, throwing on the brakes. He put fear in their hearts. It was a pure predator/prey response. He was so intense, and so quick, that even ruffed grouse would freeze and hold. It was magic.

I eventually rented a house next to a friend who had 450 acres. The grouse cycle was up and Buck would have many points in a two- or three-hour expedition. Most of the time I was hunting on my own, and as often as not the grouse would take off with a tree between us. Nevertheless, they would hold for him a long time until I arrived. I ran him in a beeper collar—one of the great bird hunting inventions of all time—from Orvis and I could hear him a couple of hundred yards away. The collar would put out a different sound when he was on point, so I knew to go to him.

I suppose this is as good a place as any to expound on the merits of pointing dogs. It is often written that the bird hunter should look for a close-working dog, typically defined as a dog that hunts between twenty and sixty yards ahead. But in reality the hunter only needs a dog to work that close in extraordinary circumstances. Yet the plodder is generally regarded as the ideal for two reasons. First, most hunters have never seen a really first-rate dog; and second, the dogs that they do hunt over simply aren't capable of pinning birds until they arrive.

It is absolutely enlightening to watch a championship shooting dog stake. Granted, you'll see dogs running too big for most hunters, but you'll also see how a dog should run: fast and smart. You'll see that birds will hold well for a dog that comes on them and surprises them. The handler normally has plenty of time to catch up to the dog, dismount, flush, and shoot for the judges.

A smart dog that is given a lot of experience will learn to handle birds under a variety of situations and will adapt his range to the cover and the method of hunting. Most of the time when I ran Buck in the grouse woods, he would hunt between 100 and 150 yards from me. When I was on horseback in more open country where I could see him for a long distance and he could see me, his range would double.

I hunted Cape May in New Jersey twice in my life for their famous woodcock migrations. The birds pile up there while waiting for a suitable wind to take them across Delaware Bay. The first time I hunted with my pal Bill Steinkraus, an Olympic gold medalist in show jumping, founding editor of Winchester Press, and one of the most interesting men I've ever known. We shot with a well-known Brittany trainer from the area and scoured the covers. Unfortunately, there were not many birds about.

The second time I hunted there, I went with two gentlemen from a sporting clay club out on Long Island who had an introduction to shoot a big farm down there. This time we were right in the middle of it. Birds were everywhere, and because of the density of the woods and the density of the birds, Buck was hunting fifty to seventy-five yards out. These gents kept complaining that he was just running too big. On one point toward the end of the day, he locked up and we flushed and quickly shot a woodcock. But even though I tapped him on the head for the retrieve, he refused to move. Walking around him I put up another bird. Again he refused to move. This kept going on until after the ninth flush, when he finally started retrieving the birds. It was one of the great moments of my bird shooting life. But I don't think those gentlemen appreciated what they had witnessed.

The *raison d'etre* of a pointing dog is to find and hold birds that the shooter would not stumble upon and flush anyway. So the only reason a pointing dog would need to stay within gunshot range is if he cannot hold his birds—never a good thing.

Obviously, the man who hunts quail off horseback or from a jeep needs a dog that runs bigger than the grouse and woodcock hunter. Really good dogs are able to adapt to the cover and the situation, but certainly there is a genetic aspect to range. Yet even the dog that works fairly close, and by fairly close I mean fifty to a hundred yards, should nevertheless hunt hard and fast.

A serious rig at a great wild quail shoot in Florida. Dogs ride in kennels below the shooter's seat, with access from the rear. My setter, Buck, waits to be loaded.

There are some specific situations where the dog does need to hunt very close and tight. I used to shoot at the Clove Valley Rod & Gun Club in New York once or twice a year with my friend Jack Hennessey. Jack had setters I had found for him; very good dogs but not really right for the conditions there. The club's fields had long strips of sorghum, perhaps twenty yards wide and a couple of hundred yards long. Jack wanted his dog to stay within the sorghum strips. But Roman was just too powerful a dog for that. What Jack really needed was a springer spaniel trained to quarter within the confines of the cover just ahead of the gun. This would have been more effective for the ground over which Jack hunted and also more sporting. When a pheasant is well pinned by a pointing dog there is a tendency to shoot it too close. But since the shooter doesn't know the exact moment when the spaniel will flush the bird, and because the spaniel is probably a short way out, the shot itself is typically more interesting.

One day when hunting at Clove Valley, I let Buck out to relieve himself while I put my gun together. I didn't pay attention

Champion Cowboys Footsteps showing form in all-age competition.

to him for a few minutes and suddenly he was gone. It was a snowy day, which made it very hard to spot a dog that was all white except for one orange ear. After five or ten minutes I gave up and began hunting with my companions. Twenty or thirty minutes later we came to a desiccated cornfield just beyond the area where I had been searching for Buck. There he was—locked on point, a cock bird hiding. No wonder he hadn't come when I called.

This wasn't the first time something like this had happened. I once owned a dog called Cowboys Footsteps that won, among other things, the Canadian Open Shooting Dog Championship. He was handled by Dave Grubb, and I had traveled down to Alabama to watch him run in some trials. We took him out hunting with Buck, who had flown down with me. Buck soon disappeared in a small pine plantation, and after we followed the other dog for ten minutes, we decided to go back and search for him. Of course, we found him locked on a covey of quail. We had passed within fifteen feet of him the first time through, but we couldn't see him through the thick government-sponsored pine forest.

It sometimes takes a dog a while to comprehend the smells of different gamebirds; but usually not too long. Buck had been trained on grouse and woodcock, yet he instantly made the transition to pheasant.

Nearly twenty years ago I traveled halfway across the country to Oklahoma to take a Delmar Smith bird dog clinic and to write a story for *Pointing Dog Journal*. Like all the faithful hunters before me, I arrived in Oklahoma City with my dog in tow. Delmar was waiting for me at the gate. I was greeted by a face that I had known for thirty years, though I had never met the man. It was a face that had stared out at me for decades from *American Field,* the journal every field trialer reads. It was a face that could have been stamped "Made in America."

Smith was simply one of the most likable men I'd ever met. He easily started conversations with total strangers; something that, as a New Yorker, I am not completely familiar or comfortable with. I'm not even sure I comprehend the concept.

It was raining so hard that we worked inside. Delmar showed me his now-famous method for teaching dogs to retrieve—force breaking with a toe pinch. He started by placing each dog he was going to work with at about six-foot intervals along a chain, called the chain gang. The dogs lie, sit, or stand as they prefer. It quiets them and they learn to give in and accept the training. "It's sort of like putting a little kid at his desk in school," according to Delmar. It gets the dog ready to work.

One English pointer bitch remained bug-eyed. She had never been worked and she just wouldn't calm down. Delmar moved her to a short chain attached to a wall. She couldn't move much and soon gave in. When she quieted Delmar put her on the table, stroking her down the right side then the left. He worked each side all the way from her ear to her rear foot. It was a bonding process that Delmar learned when he was breaking horses as a young boy of, so the story goes, eight.

When the weather cleared Delmar and I took my dog, Buck, and three of his dogs to one of the many ranches on which he had permission to run and train dogs. On the release Buck took off like a rocket. He had never seen country like this before, but he knew that birds are found along the edges so he hunted from one to another as Delmar and I walked along chewing the fat.

Buck bumped the first quail he smelled—his first ever. But he handled the second covey pretty well, and by the third he was handling them like he'd done it all his life. He went on point again and I walked ahead to flush while Delmar styled him up. I walked thirty yards but kicked up nothing. I returned and released him by tapping him lightly on the head. He immediately ran a full seventy-five yards and relocated the covey. I was as proud as if he'd just been accepted at Harvard.

COMMANDS

The bird dog does not need to know a lot of commands, but he must respond accurately and consistently to the ones he is taught. He should react immediately to "heel" or "sit," which does not need to be followed with "stay" since a dog should sit until released. He should know "kennel" for getting in a crate and jumping into a vehicle; he should know "ho" to turn, to be steady or stop on the word "whoa," to come when called "here," to spot birds when you say "mark," to hunt an area carefully for a downed bird when you say "steady," to "fetch" on command, to release the bird into your hand at the word "dead," and to be released himself on "all right" or with a tap on the head. These terms are not carved in stone, of course; the most important thing is that they do not sound like the dog's name or each other.

The above commands should all be taught during yard work, which is best done away from actual hunting areas. If you can devote two sessions a day, perhaps before and after work, to working with your dog you can accomplish all of the above fairly quickly. Dogs have a short attention span, so it is best to keep the training sessions brief. Fifteen to twenty minutes is probably the maximum. Then they should have at least an hour off before the next lesson.

The best way for a dog to learn where to find birds is through experience afield. Although it is not legal to shoot birds out of

Dogs this stylish while point and backing are a joy to behold. Mel and John
Pfeifle of Hampshire Kennels and Nancy C. Whitehead Photographer

season, there is no reason in the world not to run your dog
throughout the year, except when female gamebirds are with
eggs or broods or where prohibited by state or local law.

It is always a good idea to hunt your dog at different times of
the day. That way he will learn what type of cover birds prefer at
any given time.

GUNS AND LOADS

How you hunt the cover in which you shoot, as well as the species
of bird and the breed of dog, will affect your choice of the ideal
shotgun. I prefer double-barrel guns in the field for two reasons.
They are safer (although the shooter matters more than the gun)
and they handle better, especially after a long day. Of course, I
can only be general in my recommendations, as choosing the
best upland gun is a personal preference.

Small birds need less shot to bring them down. A quail,
woodcock, or snipe takes much less killing than a pheasant. For

the first three species, I would say the 28-gauge is ideal, or perhaps a 20-gauge with a light load. I prefer No. 7½ shot to No. 8. It has more downrange energy and penetration if a longer shot is required. If you're shooting birds at very close range, woodcock in thick woods, for instance, where you will probably only get one shot at the bird at a distance of roughly ten to twenty-five yards, skeet or cylinder chokes are best.

If you shoot pheasants over a dog that will hold the bird for a long time, cylinder or improved cylinder is probably right for the first shot and modified for the second. If birds break on you at greater distance or if you hunt over a flushing dog, improved cylinder or modified followed by full choke is probably appropriate. Twelve-gauge is the most common for this shooting, and I prefer No. 6 shot early in the year, No. 5 later on, and No. 4s if they are breaking well in front. Twenty-gauge will also do quite a good job except on the longest birds. Remember that a lot of birds are shot from behind, so penetration through to the vitals is the key to bringing them down humanely.

If you, like most upland gunners, shoot a variety of birds under a variety of conditions and are limited to one shotgun, I would suggest the 20-gauge. I would choke it improved cylinder and modified, and if I were shooting in the woods I would use a felt wad and a faster load to open up the pattern. While nothing kills as well as a 12-gauge, it is too much gun for quail in most situations and too much gun to carry through the alder thickets all day long. Some people feel that a smaller gun is more sporting, but there is actually minimal truth in this statement. The difference is just that there will be more pellets—a denser and wider pattern—with a 12-gauge. This translates to fewer crippled birds and more cleanly killed birds. To kill cleanly is the true test of sportsmanship. Small-gauge guns do have narrower dense cores (width of pattern, a.k.a. less margin for error). Except in expert hands for small birds at close range, the little .410 has limited application in the game field. Indeed, great shots can kill driven pheasant at respectable range with a 28-gauge or even a .410, but they consistently center their targets.

If I were forced to shoot just one gun for ducks and geese as well as upland game, and if I shot a fair amount of waterfowl, I would definitely choose a 12-gauge. If I shot upland birds 80 to 90 percent of the time and just pursued waterfowl on rare occasions I would probably choose a 20-gauge with three-inch chambers. To kill well and humanely, especially on geese, I would use Hevi-Shot. A 20 is light for geese most of the time, and in the hands of most shooters. Hevi-Shot is offered by Remington in size B and No. 2 in 12-gauge, but the largest offered in 20-gauge is No. 4, which would only be suitable for small species of geese that are decoying well.

HUNTING ATTIRE

After dog and gun, the most important item of gear is the boot. It is impossible to be a happy hunter without happy feet. My first pair of boots were Russell Bird Shooters, in relative terms a much more expensive acquisition in the 1960s than now. They were nevertheless very comfortable and served me well until I outgrew them. When I went north to Canada I found that a warm, insulated boot was necessary. If memory serves, it was a Danner, insulated and with heavy Vibram lug soles. Just the ticket.

As I now shoot primarily in wet climates—i.e., the British Isles—I generally use tall rubber boots from Hunter, the classic British company. If I hunted down South in dry conditions or in early fall in the Northeast, I would probably use Gokeys, perhaps in a snake-proof version (available from Orvis). High-top Brogues, also available from Orvis, have been my favorite shoes for driven shoots when wet conditions did not mandate the use of rubber. They give great ankle support and have a hard toe—lots of protection. They are also outstanding for many upland shoots and perfect in the dove field.

Now that feet are out of the way, I will head north to the head and work my way back down. While I must admit that I'm not a big fan of blaze orange in the woods, as most of the time I hunt on my own in areas where I'm unlikely to encounter someone else, I do appreciate that in some circumstances it greatly enhances safety. If blaze orange is required by law in your area, or if it makes sense because of the way you hunt, I would say that the hat is probably the most easily seen item of clothing. For the sake of this discussion, though, let us presume that orange is not a consideration.

One of my favorite hats is the simple tweed cap typically sported by Englishmen, often shown in old movies worn by boulevardiers as they drove about in their ragtop Morgans. This hat keeps the head warm, and as it is made of wool this trait holds even in wet conditions. My other favorite hat is made by Filson. It's a broad-beamed job of a waterproof fabric that keeps my bare scalp dry most of the time. It also comes with a strap that ties up under the chin, which is handy on windy days.

It is very important that shooters wear eye protection at all times, particularly in the uplands. For example, a pellet could ricochet off a branch as you or a companion shoot at grouse or a branch could slap you in the eye. I prefer wraparound glasses.

My favorite choice for a jacket again depends on the conditions. Call me old-fashioned, but I really like the old Barbour-style jacket for moderate temperatures and wet conditions. Nothing is more appropriate for European or British shooting, and this jacket works well in varied shooting conditions in America. And the venerable Barbour has recently transformed its outstanding range from waxed coats to more modern numbers, including some really handsome, comfortable, and practical tweeds.

For a number of years my favorite jacket in cool to cold weather was made by Woolrich. It's a dandy coat, preserving the muted shades I prefer in the woods. It is also quiet, warm, and tough, yet with plenty of freedom of movement for a good swing. It has enough pockets for carrying shells but doesn't provide a game bag, so this issue must be addressed. I sometimes just use a looped carrier that attaches to a belt.

The best classic American upland coat is the Ventile model from Orvis. Ventile's design has been proven in a wide range of conditions from hot to cold, dry to wet. Performance is excellent due to a combination of fiber, yarn, and weaves. The folks at Orvis tell me that Ventile is woven using 30 percent more yarn than other cotton fabrics. This dense weave makes the material waterproof, windproof, thorn-proof, and extremely durable. It is also breathable and quiet in the field. The only possible drawback is its price.

Shooting pants come in many varieties; my favorites have always been double-faced for added protection against thorns and brambles. While I have yet to try it, BUZZ OFF cloth from Orvis is supposed to protect one against biting insects, particularly ticks and mosquitoes in upland cover. (You can also spray boots and pants with permethrin.) In these days of widespread Lyme disease they are definitely worth trying.

Thin leather gloves are my favorite early in the season, especially on dry days. Something warm, ideally with a slit trigger finger, is my choice for shooting later in the season. I generally carry a knife and a multi-tool, both from Kershaw. All my day gear, including dog beeper collars, gun oil, first-aid kit, and so on, is kept in a multi-pocketed small bag. This way, I am less likely to forget anything.

Chapter
2

WATERFOWL SHOOTING

I have been very fortunate to spend more time shooting ducks than anyone I know. Yet I am not what I would describe as an expert duck hunter. Let me explain the paradox. From 1996 until 2003 I co-owned and managed the shooting at Humewood Castle in Ireland. We put down roughly 12,000 ducks a year, some of which we hatched and some of which we bought as day-olds. Although we did this shooting on a commercial basis, we also saved much shooting for ourselves and our friends. It was a spectacular shoot that received rave reviews in England in *The Shooting Times* and *The Shooting Gazette* and in the United States in the *Bird Hunting Report* and *Shooting Sportsman*. Humewood was considered by most cognoscenti as the preeminent duck shoot in the British Isles.

The birds were put out on the lakes before they could fly. The pen had no top on it, and it was actually designed more to keep predators out than to keep the birds in. An electric wire was placed around each pen to keep fox and mink at bay. (Normally, over a hundred foxes were culled each year.) Young ducks imprint, and because the game keeper took care of them from day

Decoys that add motion attract more ducks.
Photo courtesy of Wing Wavers, Inc.

one they thought he was Mother. When he whistled they came, often by the thousands. It was an amazing sight to watch the ducks walk from the lake in a line that stretched for four hundred yards to the game crop where he fed them. Because they were free to fly, they did as soon as they could. Thanks to this exercise and the lack of confinement they flew at virtually the same speed as wild mallards.

Often they would fly off for many hours. It was sort of scary to see $200,000 worth of ducks disappear. Fortunately, there were few lakes near our shoot so they always did come back. The main reason they returned was for the food. (We did lose a thousand ducks once late in the season, when the remnants of a hurricane came by and blew them to Tipperary.)

Most years I shot something in excess of a thousand ducks, and I must admit I enjoyed every minute of it. Because of the way they were raised, they tended to present themselves at thirty-five to fifty yards over the guns. Great sport indeed. This taught me quite a lot about loads and chokes. We were very fortunate in that Ireland still allows the use of lead shot.

While I have shot geese in Iceland, graylags, Canada geese on eastern Long Island and in upstate New York, and Chilean and Magellan geese in Argentina, I must admit that I've primarily been along for the ride, most often with a guide doing all of the real work. While there is nothing more beautiful than being in a blind as the moon sets and the sun rises, there are two or three factors that have limited the amount of true wildfowl shooting I've done. Much of my life has been spent in New York City, where it is a tough enough town to keep a car in, let alone a layout boat. So I have chosen instead to take the lazy man's way out and hire a guide as needed. Thankfully, I was lucky to live near good duck hunting and very good goose shooting seventy miles to the east.

In the glory days of American waterfowling, days when market gunners would shoot carloads of ducks, there was no better area along the eastern seaboard for hunting than Long Island. Rich Park Avenue types formed clubs and bought or leased prime lands so they could hunt in gentlemanly fashion. Serious hunters designed and refined gunning boats, and masterful decoy carvers, probably unaware of the posthumous treasures they were creating, plied their craft.

But the great flocks of birds that blackened the sky and the rafts that covered the water are no more. And while the market gunners are long gone and few clubs remain, the traditions continue, both

The traditional thatched gunning boat provides a perfect and natural camouflage that also transports one back, metaphorically, to the good old days.

among decoy carvers and men who shoot from gunning boats. (Gunning boats are also referred to as layout or punting boats.)

Nearly twenty-five years ago I spent a day hunting with a guide named George Combs who, like his market-hunting great-grandfathers, used gunning boats. In the old days the men stalked large rafts of birds, killing them with punt guns and shipping the game to the finest restaurants in New York City. George and I towed the gunning boats by skiff to the western end of the Great South Bay. A great advantage of this method is flexibility. It is possible to predict where the birds will be based on weather and tide and then set up there.

Leaving the skiff anchored in deep water, we traveled in gunning boats to a small strip of land, where we set the boats in among the sea grass. George quickly set out the Canada geese decoys on one side, black ducks in the middle, and broadbills on the other side. We lay down in the boats, which were camouflaged by salt grass thatching, and waited. Buffleheads skimmed across the water well out of range. Brant (no relation to the author) frequently flew in range, but as they were protected birds we did not shoot. A black duck came out of the east and was about to land in our decoy spread when we sat up and shot. It quickly veered off and I didn't connect until the third shot. Shooting from a sitting position takes a little getting used to. The Northeast was experiencing an unseasonably warm fall that year, and it made the hunting less productive than usual. We did bag two more black ducks, the only birds that came to our decoys, and missed a long passing shot at a canvasback.

Clothing can mean the difference between an enjoyable day in the blind and enduring a frozen hell. In addition to expedition-weight long underwear, I wear insulated waders or Sorel boots depending on the hunting conditions. A warm cap is a necessity, and I often bring a ski mask on really cold days. Warm gloves are a must, as is a waterproof parka. The hunter should be as camouflaged as possible, but in snowy weather this entails wearing white instead of traditional camo.

Even in places like Long Island, you don't need to hire a guide to be successful. South Haven Park on the Carmans River in Brookhaven offers public hunting from blinds with a daily public draw. The bayside of Barrier Beach along the southern shore also offers good shooting, particularly for black ducks. But you do need a good four-wheel drive to get your trailer in and out. And a good seaworthy duck boat is essential. (By the way, my favorite book for boat and blind designs is *Successful Waterfowling*, by Zach Taylor, now out of print.)

According to various wildlife biologists with whom I've spoken, Long Island's sea duck shooting is a largely untapped resource. Access is easy from any north shore harbor into the sound. Peconic Bay also offers good shooting. White-winged scoters and old squaw predominate in the early season, but sea duck shooting is not for the amateur. Bob Hand, who was a master decoy carver from Sag Harbor and one of the most dedicated and accomplished gunners on the island, once said to me, "You've got to know the water and your equipment. The sea can look calm when you go out. Then the wind and the tide change and you get a riptide and the boat lands in your face."

The most productive wild duck shooting I've ever experienced took place just south of Buenos Aires, Argentina. Five A.M. seemed to come earlier than usual. Working on a tight schedule the day before in the province of Cordoba, we shot doves early in the day, returned to the lodge for lunch, chartered a plane to Buenos Aires, and drove another hour south to Los Patos. Dinner began at 10:00 P.M. Then into the arms of Morpheus.

By 6:00 A.M. we were outside, dressed in waders and waterfowl gear. The guides fetched our shotguns from the gun room. It was nearly a forty-minute drive to the shooting grounds, though probably only five to ten miles as the crow flies. We left the main road and turned down a dirt track pitted by too many drivers cutting cross-country when it was wet. The moon was full and very bright. A few clouds formed eerie shapes.

We arrived at the small pond, made last-minute adjustments in the darkness, and walked a hundred yards or so to a clump of grass and reeds about twenty yards wide. As my two companions, Chuck Larsen and Kirk Kelly, and I settled onto the metal stools in the blind, our guides, Brian and Paco, set out the decoys.

The area is vast and lightly hunted. Brian, who had been guiding in Argentina for four years, mentioned that there were fewer than a hundred hunters shooting the entire area. A trio of rosy-billed porchard, the most common species in the area, came in when it was still too dark to shoot. Soon, as the sun slowly rose, the action became fast and furious. Ducks came in singly, in pairs, trios, quartets, quintets; sometimes larger flocks and sometimes two separate groups coming in almost simultaneously. It was July, winter in the Southern Hemisphere. Skim ice glazed the pond's surface, but the shooting kept us warm.

Sixty percent of the ducks we saw were rosy bills, 30 percent pintails, and the remaining 10 percent were a mix of thirteen other species. During five shoots (three mornings and two afternoons) we bagged a variety of species. For collectors, the complete list of ducks observed is as follows: speckled teal, Brazilian duck, Argentine bluebill, silver teal, ringed teal, cinnamon teal, red shoveler, white-cheeked pintail, yellow-billed pintail, Chilean widgeon, white-faced whistling duck, fulvous whistling duck, and rosy bill.

Chuck was quick and accurate with his autoloader and often dropped three or more ducks out of each flight. I was limited to a maximum of two shots with my trusty over-under Perazzi. I had brought down some old lead duck loads from Federal, and although the shells must have been twenty years old they worked flawlessly. And no matter how much we shot, the ducks just kept pouring in. We had a self-imposed limit of 125 cartridges per man per session, and we were all empty by 9:00 A.M.

Something I find interesting is the different views that civilized countries have on what is and is not fair chase or good sport. In the U.K., for example, it is illegal to crate and shoot birds. While really designed as part of the ban on boxed pigeon shoots, it now makes tower releases illegal. Oddly enough, British shooters cringe at the idea of tower releases, although it is common and often done in a sporting manner at shooting clubs in North America. (The best tower that I know—it produces the tallest and fastest birds—is located in Florida, of all places. The height of the tower, coupled with a fairly strong prevailing wind, creates birds that dip and curl extremely well.) Yet British sportsmen have no qualms about night-flighting ducks or feeding ponds, both of which are considered unsporting and illegal in North America. Personally, I have no problem with either. Indeed, I will jump at the opportunity to shoot boxed pigeons in the rings of Spain, the Dominican Republic, or the United States.

Argentina has certainly been more influenced by the European sensibility, as baiting is both legal and integral to hunting. Each of the thirty ponds controlled by the Los Patos estate, where we hunted, is fed a hundred pounds of corn every two days, starting six weeks before the season.

Most of the birds decoyed well, except at one point when I became more concerned with getting photographs than staying hidden. Some pass shooting was required, but with a couple of exceptions range was not excessive and "sky busting" was never an issue. The afternoon sessions tended to provide "taller" ducks. The birds did come in from all angles, and those from directly behind—going-away, station-one skeet high-house shots—were quite interesting.

The importance of having the correct gear and paying attention to conditions when hunting waterfowl cannot be stressed enough. Indeed, the closest I ever came to dying while plying my sport—and this includes twice being charged by lions and sharing blinds with cobras and other venomous snakes—was duck hunting in Shinnecock Bay with an old-time guide named Frank Downs.

It was the last week of the season and I arrived to find the saltwater bay completely frozen. The ice had moved Frank's blind a few hundred yards and everything was encased in ice. It was no longer possible to just get into his boat and cruise out to the blind. Instead, we had to load the boat with decoys and then he pulled and I pushed across the ice. This alone wouldn't have been too bad, but the ice was not all that thick and every twenty yards or so we would plunge into the water. This was thirty years ago, before thick neoprene waders were available, so by the time we got to the blinds we were extremely cold and wet.

Frank, tough as nails, placed the decoys and every so often went out and re-broke the ice. He needn't have bothered. The only birds we saw all day were geese headed for Southampton at ten thousand feet. Nevertheless, we stayed in the blind for hours before calling it a day. It was just as bad going back as it was going out, but by that time my energy was depleted by the cold. Every step back was a struggle, and a hundred yards from shore I could feel my whole body shutting down. If this wasn't hyperthermia it was something pretty close. I'm still not sure how I forced myself to shore. My feet were so numb that I had to take off my shoes to feel the pedals for the drive back; it was a struggle to stay awake.

Goose shooting in Iceland was a fairly casual but splendid affair. Jim Dee, a public-relations man for one of the gun companies, used to organize combination trips for salmon and graylag goose shooting on the Langa River, a couple of hours from Reykjavik. The goose shooting was very good in that there were a lot of birds about. It was only so-so in that the guides were at best marginal at placing decoys, and if memory serves they didn't call at all. So roughly half the birds we shot came into the decoys and the rest were quite long passing shots. In the light of the long midnight sun, sleep was minimal. We would fish till ten or eleven at night and be up again to get to the goose blinds between three and four in the morning.

The exact opposite of the casual shooting in Iceland was the shooting provided at a grand old club called Ottawa on the southern shores of Lake Erie. I shot there with my great friend Tom Roulston, who has been a member for many years. The club itself has been going since the 1860s. It is limited to twenty-five or so members, determined by the number of bedrooms at the club. Each member has his own guide, referred to as a "punter," as in the old days they did actually use punt boats.

Obviously, they adhere to all fish and game regulations and therefore do not bait. They do, however, encourage ducks to come to their area by constantly improving habitat and also by planting corn and other crops for the birds to feed upon.

In 2003, I shot there with Tom about a week after the season opened. We made our way to the far side of the club, where we were going to shoot that afternoon with Tom's punter, Mike Koppleman, who already had a boat loaded with decoys. We traveled the waterways, best described as irrigation canals, and used specially designed rails to move the boat from one canal to another, which kept the portages fairly simple. We were going to hunt an area where there was no blind, so we merely hid among the reeds and sat on stools. Mike was a master at placing decoys and calling, and it wasn't long before the ducks started to move.

Remote
Control Kit

Different companies have created various models of decoys with mechanical motion. The action of the wings is seen by waterfowl and gets the birds' attention. Photo courtesy of Open Zone, Inc.

We were in the thick of it virtually every day—mallards, teal, widgeon, and wood ducks all came to our decoys. Tom and Mike like to use oversize decoys and lots of them. Their secret weapons are a couple of oversize decoys set high on stakes with flapping and rotating wings. Robo-ducks!

On days two and three we shot out of a classic blind built into one of the small embankments along a swamp. It was good to great shooting, and after the high-volume days spent on the dove fields of South America, pheasant shoots in the British Isles, and partridge in Spain, it taught me a wonderful lesson: You don't have to kill a lot of birds to have a spectacular day. This was one of my all-time favorite shoots. The area was pristine, and both of my companions were true sportsmen. In three days of hunting we shot our limit every day without once shooting each other's birds. Tom noted that in all his years of duck shooting that had never happened before.

This was my first hunt using Hevi-Shot, made by Remington. To say it is great stuff is a huge understatement. It kills as well or better than lead.

The only problem I experienced was that the bolt handle on the autoloader Tom had lent me came off after the second day's shoot. It was lost in the marsh, which wasn't a big deal for us as Tom had brought along a spare gun, but it shows the importance of prior planning. This is actually a fairly common mishap with autoloaders, undoubtedly the most frequent after jamming, which is usually caused by poor cleaning. You should always buy a spare bolt handle when you purchase this type of shotgun, as it only costs a couple of bucks. If you know how to replace it—generally just pushing it in until it clicks—you might save a trip.

Into the 1970s and early '80s I often went goose shooting in Southampton. There was a humble potato farmer named Phil Downs, whose farm was right behind the Southampton diner on the Montauk Highway. (I say "humble" because he had a couple of hundred acres of some of the most valuable land in the country, which he sold off as a real estate development for mucho dinero.) Phil had installed pit blinds, and the geese would come from Mecox Bay at first light.

It was only a couple of hours from New York City and the shooting was usually outstanding. The only problem was that the geese had usually fed too long on mollusks and were not great eating. So I switched my shooting to upstate New York. Here the geese were largely corn fed, and today I would guess that with the increased goose numbers the shooting is equal to or better than in the Hamptons.

I once went down to Maryland's Eastern Shore, fabled for its goose shooting, with George Gruenefeld, who was the outdoor writer for the *Montreal Gazette*. I can't say we had bad luck; rather, we had no luck at all. But we still had a good time. Shooting can be just as much about camaraderie as birds killed.

CANINE COMPANIONS

Many of my best friends in the sporting life have been dogs, either English setters or Labrador retrievers. In 1997, shortly after I moved to Ireland, a wonderful woman named Clare de Burgh, a well-known breeder and field trialer, told me to call Shane O'Toole about a recent litter of puppies out of his great international champion. Shane has competed internationally as a field trialer and is a highly rated judge.

When I arrived to see the pups I also found that he had a nine-month-old dog, lovingly treated and well started. Dusty did not work long term for Shane because she was too antsy to make a proper trial dog. She was out of Clare's breeding, a lovely medium-yellow dog typical of the line. We took to each other instantly, and Shane brought her out to Humewood Castle a few days later to show her in action. She sat and heeled and jumped back into the car on command. She also responded to hand signals—left, right, and back. We walked with her for a little ways and flushed and shot three or four pheasants, which she brought nicely to hand. She was a remarkable dog for her age. Needless to say, Shane left and Dusty stayed. I found out years later from Clare that Shane quite regretted selling the dog as he was very fond of her. He'd put a tremendous effort into the young pup and did so with a knowledgeable and soft hand.

But he was right that she wasn't going to make a good field trial dog. My three other Labs all sit forever waiting for the command to retrieve. Not Dusty. Shoot the gun and unless she's tied down she's off like a rocket. Yet if my life depended on one of my dogs bringing back a runner, seen or blind, Dusty is the one I would pick.

On one occasion we were observing the shooting at Coolattin, a medium-quality pheasant shoot about twenty minutes from our property, and I decided to bring her along for a little bit of work. With a driven pheasant shoot, most of the retrieving is done when the drive is over. On this particular drive a serious number of birds were shot. I sent her out for a bird, crippled and running about 150 yards away. Seventy-five yards into the cast she spotted the runner. Even though there were numerous dead birds between her and her prey she stayed with him. A lovely job.

We shot a lot of ducks at Humewood; our best day was 907 to eight guns. (Don't think it was easy, though, as it took roughly five thousand cartridges to accomplish the task.) Dusty loved this, the only problem being that after a while she thought she didn't have to go very far into the lake to find birds. One day on the second drive a dead drake mallard lay near the reeds on the far side, two or three hundred yards away. She didn't see the bird go down, so she swam out twenty-five yards, looked around, saw nothing, and came back. Three tries and I couldn't get her to go farther. In frustration, I took her to the end of the dock, pointed her in the right direction, and tossed her. (There was no roughness or cruelty involved.) Being a smart dog, she got the idea and swam all the way to the bird. After that, when I sent her for a long bird she believed me. (Never lie to your dog!)

Dusty is also an outstanding upland hunter and has put up numerous pheasant and a few woodcock for me. She doesn't tear game, and while her favorite thing in the world is hunting, her second favorite is sitting on my lap in front of our roaring fire in the library.

Renata, my better half, decided that she too wanted a dog. Back to Clare de Burgh, who this time heard that Frank Mansell, one of Ireland's preeminent springer trainers and field trialers, had a fabulous Labrador who under the pressure of competition would "make a voice." (To the best of my understanding, this is not considered a fault in North America but causes an immediate elimination in Great Britain.) Otherwise, Darky was perfect. Frank brought him to us on a day when we had a shoot going. We saw him work and he showed us how he trained him. Interestingly, Frank trains all his dogs at a whisper. His thought process is a good one: At a hundred yards the shout is going to sound like a whisper so if you have to raise your voice when the dog is close he's probably going to ignore you when far away.

Soon after Darky came to us he stopped making the noise when on peg. He was a young dog, and as Frank readily admitted, he just tried to make him too fast and put too much pressure on him. Although a tiger in the field, Darky took a few days to adjust to Renata and me and it was months before he was comfortable with strangers. Now he loves everyone and is the undisputed boss of the castle. Handsome and athletic before he got old, he always hit the water hard and fast, leaping feet into the air like one of those dogs competing on ESPN. By the way, Darky is a common name in Ireland for black Labradors and is not meant pejoratively. After all, in that country's homogeneous society there is no one to offend.

Then there was Maggie. John, a friend of ours from Pennsylvania, saw our great Irish Labs and decided that he wanted one as well. I called Frank Mansell, who had a lovely though quite expensive bitch. She had won a couple of field trials and was capable of winning more; the only problem being that Frank had half a dozen springers in contention for championships and couldn't justify taking the days away for the single Labrador that he was campaigning. John decided he would buy the dog. Then he thought that it would be great if we bred her to Darky and gave him a couple of pups from the litter. That was the plan, anyway. But after Maggie had been with us until she went into season and then weaned the puppies, she simply had become part of our family and there was no way to let her go. We refunded John's money and gave him two puppies.

GUNS AND LOADS

Here are my general guidelines for waterfowling guns and loads. (There is much more information on chokes and loads later in the book.)

For pass shooting mallards No. 4 lead, which is no longer legal, was excellent. If the birds are at a distance I would definitely make Hevi-Shot my first choice these days, with tungsten/iron my second, and steel third. Bismuth would be a distant fourth. Consider that steel is lighter than lead for the same size, so you need to go up in size to have a pellet of the same weight. For example, No. 4 lead equates to No. 2 steel. Number 5 or No. 6 lead was ideal for decoyed ducks, so just make the appropriate adjustment if you want to go to steel.

If there are lots of teal and other small ducks in the mix, and few mallards or other large wildfowl, No. 6 is a fine choice. Number 2s were my choice in the pre-steel days for decoying geese, and BBs for pass shooting.

I suppose that I have killed more ducks with an over-under Perazzi 12-gauge than anything else. If I were shooting a fair amount of wildfowl and primarily using steel, I would definitely step up to a 3- or 3½-inch 12-gauge. To absorb the recoil, and to get a third shot, I would recommend an autoloader. I have made this switch myself. These days I'm shooting a 3½-inch Beretta, and I have gone whole hog with it.

Beretta's AL391 Urika Max-4 HD is a tough, durable, and reliable shotgun, perfect for the harshest conditions and the most demanding wildfowler. Without modification, it will handle normal loads or 3½-inch, two-ounce loads. The over-bored barrel provides excellent patterning characteristics, and the stock is adjustable for drop and cast. Lastly, it is a camouflaged model, which makes it less likely to spook game.

Camouflaged shotguns such as this Beretta are the bee's knees in a duck blind. Photo courtesy of Beretta

Chapter

3

FORWARD ALLOWANCE

Perception is a funny thing. Color-blindness is an obvious example. What looks red to one individual seems green to another. But even for two non-color-blind human beings it is impossible to know definitively that each sees red in exactly the same way. So it is with lead, or forward allowance.

One person may judge lead in terms of bird lengths, another in terms of feet, and still another in terms of a gap as seen off the barrels. Even for two shooters who judge lead by a measurement in feet, one individual's perception of four feet might seem more like six feet to the other.

A number of years ago CNN ran a story on vision-altering goggles. The lenses were adjusted so that everything looked a few feet to the left of its actual position. Quarterbacks were asked to wear them and throw footballs to receivers. Their first few attempts failed, but after a while the subconscious mind took over and the passers were able to hit their mark. Interestingly, once honed in, the new lead prevailed. When they were again allowed to throw the football without wearing the glasses, there was

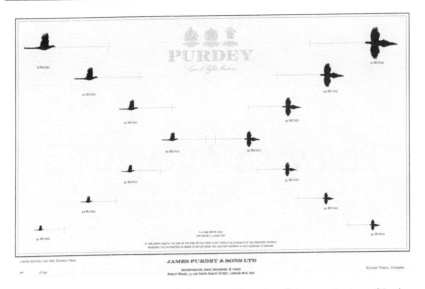

This chart shows the relative size of pheasants at varying distances. Courtesy of Purdey

a corresponding shift to the other side. After a while, this corrected itself. Ain't the unconscious grand?

We'll delve into the mechanics of shooting in the next chapter on clay games, which are a great way to learn and practice shots you'll often see in the field, but first let's look at a single critical element: the sight picture. One of the keys to consistently killing birds is to find a sight picture that works and memorize it. A common failing is to try to make things better. That just doesn't work. There's an old story, which may or may not be apocryphal, about a mediocre shot who suddenly became an ace on archangels. (Archangel is an English term used to describe extremely tall pheasant on a driven shoot, those birds up in the stratosphere.) His friends were mystified. Eventually he admitted, "I finally saw the sight picture."

There are four primary methods for developing lead, or forward allowance: (1) swing through; (2) instinctive; (3) pull away; and (4) maintained or sustained. Some types of shots are better taken with one method than the others.

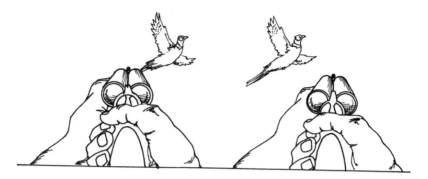

With "swing through" less lead is seen than in maintained lead. The farther away the bird is from the shooter, the more "air" must be seen before slapping the trigger. While not ideal for all situations, swing through is probably the easiest method of lead to learn.

As the name implies, with swing through the gun is mounted with the barrels inserted behind the target and accelerated through it. Both swing through and instinctive are very good for beginners and for those who don't have the time to become much more than an average-plus shot. There are some brilliant practitioners of both methods, of course, but I'm referring to the normally coordinated shooter who only spends a little time practicing. These methods create barrel speed, which reduces the likelihood of slowing or stopping the barrels. They also reduce the amount of perceived lead that you need to see. And both are excellent for establishing the correct line.

Because of the accelerating barrels, perhaps a bird-and-a-half-lead would appear correct, as opposed to three or four lengths for someone shooting maintained lead. The biggest drawback to swing through is that we don't always move the gun at the same speed or even accelerate it at the same speed from one shot to the next or from one day to the next. This leads to inconsistency, especially on the clay field.

With the instinctive method, the idea is to read the line and swing through from tail to head. Your barrels should be reaching the head of the bird as the gun reaches your face. Fire immediately. (I have read that Norman Clarke, a protégé of the famous Robert Churchill, did not like this explanation and felt that a *seen* lead, or sight picture, was often needed. He felt that firing immediately on shouldering was not always best.)

Avoid too much "cheek time" or you will tend to slow the gun, look at the bead, and miss. This approach, similar in a way to swing through, but with less time on the face, is very good at making a novice or poor shot quickly mediocre.

With the pull-away method you mount on the bird, matching its speed during the mounting process. You travel with it for a short distance to read the line and then accelerate—pull away—and shoot when your unconscious mind feels the lead to be correct. This creates an accelerating barrel. Many of the masters of pull away and maintained lead seem to have very little follow through, but the truth is that they do have enough—the barrels are moving until the shot has exited the barrel.

With maintained lead, you basically insert the barrels with the correct lead established during the mount. (Never let the target get in front of, or beat, your barrels.) The key is to "challenge the target," as Gary Herman calls it. You can fire as the gun hits your cheek or stay with it for a moment to confirm the correctness of the sight picture.

The drawback with maintained lead is that it is very difficult to correctly read the line on a live curling or dropping target. A shooter really needs to be able to use all styles in order to select the best method for each situation.

While I rarely shoot clays these days, I do recommend it as a useful exercise. Trigger time just cannot be beaten for developing timing, rhythm, and coordination. You can work on your gun mount and at the same time experiment with all four of the above

This is NOT an efficient waiting or ready position. If the bird were to take off to my right, the tip of the barrel would need to travel a yard or so. When possible, adopt the ready position shown elsewhere (Digweed et al). Photo courtesy of Suzan Bruner

methods. Even the humble skeet field will teach us much if we shoot it the way we shoot gamebirds.

Do you move-mount-shoot as a continuous movement or do you box your mount and then chase the bird? Do you carry your gun at port arms and have to flail before beginning your mount or do you keep the butt close to your armpit or chest with the barrels pointed in the general direction of the shot to create a smooth, compact mount? Does the tip of your barrel hardly move on a practice mount? Do you wait with your muzzles too high, thereby forcing yourself to drop the barrels and raise the butt excessively before arriving at the shoulder pocket?

Try shooting skeet doubles in reverse order—it makes you quick. It also shows how much more spread there is to the pattern

Too square a mount: The gun should be across the body at roughly a 45-degree angle and with feet close together. As posed here, both the mount and movement will suffer and recoil will be unpleasant. Also try to avoid a wide "rifleman's" stance with weight on the back foot and upper body slanted rearward from the waist. Photo courtesy of Dan Horan

with game chokes at thirty yards than at under twenty-one yards, where you most often break a skeet target. And if you're too slow on the second bird it will also teach you how to address dropping targets.

Get a friend to videotape you. (You, not the target.) Is the gun glued to your face? Is the mount compact and efficient? Does your gun get caught up on your jacket as you mount? Study your mount and look for flaws.

On a small bird such as a partridge or dove it is perfectly acceptable to look at the whole bird. For pheasants or waterfowl you should focus on the head. This way you're less likely to be fooled into making the long body and/or tail part of the sight picture, which may cause you to shoot for the middle of the bird or even farther back.

You should read (or feel) the lead off the bird, not off the barrel as some trap shots tend to do. You should not, as some suggest, see some imaginary moving point in the air a few feet in front of the target and "concentrate" vision there. Indeed, there are times when everything is a bit blurry or "seen" as a halftone. For instance, on low skeet at station six (except for flyers or trap, I

This was an interesting clay presentation with quartering birds from left to right. The recoil from taking the rear, and lower, bird first put me nearly on the correct line for the leading target.

always shoot low gun) when I mount the gun the barrels obscure the target. Both the target and barrels appear blurred. After forty years of taking this shot, I read, or feel, this as correct and slap the trigger.

When I'm not shooting much, maybe at the beginning of the season, and my normal method for tall (high) birds isn't working, I switch to swing through. I do this to increase my lead while at the same time establishing the correct line. I still, of course, see a gap—not reading off the barrels—on tall birds before I fire. But this rapidly accelerating barrel makes it much easier to connect. The taller the bird, the greater the need for acceleration. I'm not as consistent this way as when things are really working for my own style, but it's a better, safer choice when I need to shoot into form.

Chapter
4

CLAY GAMES AND
SHOOTING METHOD

C lay target games—skeet, trap, and sporting clays—can be viewed in one of two ways: as serious competition or just great fun. It is the perfect way for the game shooter to get in some practice during the off-season, and it's especially important for honing your skills just before the season begins.

Shooters who pursue each game seriously need special equipment, regular practice sessions, and good fundamentals. The beauty of each sport for the competitor is that each shooter is classified according to skill level. The skeet or trap shooter who scores in the high eighties, for example, shoots in separate classes and for separate prizes than the shooter with a ninety-eight average. This allows the shooter to work up the ladder without becoming discouraged.

To compete at the highest level, first-class equipment is a must. But it need not be excessively expensive. The 12-gauge autoloader is highly competitive on the skeet range. But to shoot it well at skeet, your gun may need some tweaking. Gunfit is critical, as is a crisp trigger. Chokes of skeet or cylinder are required, and the serious shooter will pattern his gun to know point of impact and which brand of ammo it shoots best. (All of these elements are discussed in detail in subsequent chapters.)

Each game is dealt with separately here, but much of what I am writing about skeet is relevant to the other games so I suggest that you at least skim the entire section.

Glasses should be worn at all times when participating in clay games. The most important reason is to protect the eyes, so the lens material must be able to absorb impact from pellets. Glasses will also protect you from flying bits of clay or burnt powder. Various colors help your visual acuity in specific conditions. If you wear prescription lenses it is very important to get your glasses made by someone who understands the needs of the shooter. When you shoot you simply aren't looking through the glasses the same way as you do at other times. Specifically, you are not looking straight ahead, and even the best shooter's head will be rotated somewhat down and slightly to the right. This means that you're looking high and to the left through your glasses. (See chapter 11, Safety and Etiquette, for more information.)

MY TEN COMMANDMENTS FOR SHOOTING

The basics of stance and correct shooting form are discussed throughout this chapter in relation to specific shots offered by each clay game, but here is my best advice for all types of shooters.

1. The eyes are quicker than the hands. Where the eyes go, the hands will follow.
2. The gun mount isn't just important to the shot, it is the shot.
3. Barrel speed kills birds.
4. Twist from the waist to keep the barrels on the same plane as the target.

5. Focus only on the target (never double-check your barrel or your bead).
6. The only target that counts is the one you're shooting at right now.
7. When you break a target, especially a difficult one, memorize the lead.
8. Be confident, be relaxed, be focused.
9. If the gun don't fit, you just won't hit.
10. If you aren't a safe shot nothing else matters.

SKEET

I started shooting skeet when I was still a teenager, although I never shot competitively except at the club level. While at college I belonged to two clubs where I was able to practice regularly. Coaching was not common then, so the little I knew about skeet came from a book written by Barney Hartman, *Hartman on Skeet.* My scores were less than breathtaking, at least in part due to the fact that I tended to shoot my game gun, which was choked

Classic form on the skeet field: Note gun at about 45 degrees across the body with the weight on the front foot. It is a good picture of relaxed concentration.

improved cylinder and modified. My margin of error was quite limited. Also, I was a swing-through shooter back then and started my barrels too close to each trap house.

Roughly twenty-five years ago I took a clinic offered by Ed Scherer, a top coach of his day. He added a discipline and a routine that allowed my scores to climb. Key among these was the hold point.

The hold point that Scherer described was perhaps twenty feet out from each trap house. He would place a stack of clays about a foot high at that point as a marker. The idea was to mount the gun on the center stake, come up to the right height, move the gun back to the hold point, and then call for the target. The shooter would look back toward the house, but not as far as the house; rather, at the point where the bird first appears.

As I mostly use skeet, and to a lesser extent sporting clays, as a discipline to keep myself in practice for game shooting, I still go through this routine. But when I come back to the hold point I dismount my gun and place the top of the butt just below my armpit. The preferred hold point for each individual is different, depending on the shooter's barrel speed and the speed of reflexes. I suggest that you stand on each station without a gun to see where you are first able to view each target. That is where you should look for the bird. The hands are not as quick as the eyes, so it makes sense to start the barrels farther toward the center stake than your sight point. Whether you should hold, say, five or twenty feet closer to the center stake is something that you will have to determine by trial and error.

When I refer to sight point, I do not mean that you should take a hard focus there. Instead, keep your eyes in that direction with a soft focus that allows the target to come into your peripheral vision; then lock onto it.

Footwork is one of the true keys to shooting well. All too often I see shooters with their legs way too far apart. Ideally, your heels should be no farther apart than your shoulders, and depending on an individual's conformation, heels can be as close together as six to nine inches. The front knee should be slightly bent, with the weight slightly toward the front foot. Fifty-five to 60 percent of the weight should be on the front foot. The toe of the leading foot should be pointed where you plan to break the target.

It is twenty-one yards from each station to the center stake. The target should be broken just before or just after the stake, depending on how quick you are and other variables like wind. In doubles, try to get the first target early so the second target can also be shot near the stake. If you take the second bird late it may appear to be a much easier target, but the width of the pattern is narrow, which makes for a smaller margin of error.

One of the keys to target shooting, indeed to all shooting, and too rarely exhibited except by top shots, is twisting from the waist. Too often, shooters sway or shift weight from one foot to the next. This is plain wrong. For one thing, it makes it too easy to come off the correct line. You must learn to twist, or to pivot, from the waist. The easiest way to get a feel for this movement is to practice a common exercise for calisthenics: Take a broom handle or something similar and place it behind your neck, holding it toward the ends. Then stand in front of a mirror with your feet directly below your shoulders and twist to the left and the right. This is the way to move to a target. Now pick up your shotgun, double-checking that it is empty, of course, and practice moving to the left and the right by twisting from the waist in the same way.

Ed Anderson, a truly outstanding shot who is also the gunsmith of the Beretta Gallery in Manhattan, once said something

G.T. Herman was the former chief shooting instructor for the USSCA. Here he shows exemplary form while waiting for an incoming partridge-type presentation.

along this line that was really quite enlightening. I knew it on an unconscious level, but I had never heard it verbalized before: The mount *is* the shot. Truer words, at least in regard to clay shooting, which is what we were discussing, were never spoken. The mount starts with good footwork (described above), but as you see the target you move the barrels toward it, blending the two until the proper sight picture is established.

In this mounting process, the head must remain still and the eyes should be close to level. (To keep one's eyes level, the gunfit must be perfect.) In an ideal mounting process, the tip of the barrels seem to hardly move at all. The gun finds the face and shoulder pocket at almost the same time.

There is a perfect pocket, just inside the shoulder, which is actually quite easy to feel. Raise your right arm, keeping it bent at the elbow and parallel to the ground. Now move it forward slightly. You can use your left hand to feel the pocket described. This is where the butt plate should be placed. Whether the top of the butt is level with the top of this pocket or a bit below will depend on your physical conformation. Do not lower your face to the gun. (One common mistake includes mounting on the top of the bicep or point of the shoulder—ouch!) Some shooters will find the pocket more easily by standing square to the gun. However, in shooting situations it is generally best to have the gun going across your body at about a 45-degree angle. You must learn to find this pocket with an unmounted gun for all disciplines except skeet and trap.

The gun needs to be locked into this pocket. This can be accomplished in two ways, and one is not necessarily better than the other. The elbow can be brought quite high, just above the vertical, which locks the butt in place by the interaction of the bones. Or the elbow can be rotated down so that the muscles lock the butt in place.

The left arm should be held at a naturally comfortable angle. Keeping it parallel to the ground will quickly exhaust the arm. Keeping it directly below the gun, as the shooter does in rifle shooting, just doesn't work for shotgunning. A 30- to 45-degree angle below the horizontal is about right.

Every shooter's style and technique differs slightly. After you've spent enough time shooting, you will eventually develop your own natural style and technique. Always try to keep it based on sound fundamentals. That is the key.

Shooting all birds at the earliest possible moment is a great advantage. For one thing, you should be able to break them before they slow and start to drop. For another, on a windy day, the quicker you break them the easier they are most of the time. On incomers, your pattern has a much greater spread at twenty or twenty-five yards than it does at ten yards. The great skeet expert Lee Braun recommended shooting the incomer on doubles much closer than I typically do.

Because skeet targets are thrown in a consistent pattern along a consistent line and at a consistent speed, they naturally lend themselves to shooting maintained/sustained lead. As soon as you see the target, regardless of whether you shoot gun up or gun down, start to move the gun. If you are shooting gun down, blend the barrels to the target with the lead established during the mounting process. It is this consistency of target and discipline that allows most competitive shooters to score such high numbers of perfect rounds in competition.

In skeet, as in all shooting, you don't need a lot of follow through, just enough to allow the shot to exit the barrel. If you don't double-check your sights, follow through is normally not an issue as the gun won't stop. However, some shooters start to shoot the second bird of the pair before the first one is broken, destroying their follow through. Break the first bird, consciously follow through in the beginning, and then go to the second bird.

Targets at the skeet field are normally shot at extremely close range; twenty-five yards should be the maximum. At that range No. 9 shot still has enough energy to consistently break a spinning clay target. (Beyond twenty-five yards No. 8s have significantly more energy.) The combination of skeet or cylinder choke and No. 9 shot produces the widest pattern, one dense enough to keep any reasonably well-centered clay from flying through unscathed. (It's a different world with the little .410, though.)

Consistency is the key in this game. Unless there is some external factor at play, such as gusting wind, you should always try to shoot exactly the same way each time. This is what leads to great scores. It is also important to stay relaxed yet focused. This focus doesn't need to last long; really just from the moment before you call for the bird until it is broken (or in the case of doubles, until both are broken).

Krieghoff guns have a great reputation both on skeet fields, as shown here, and in competitive trap. The trigger is mechanical, not inertia driven. Photo courtesy of Krieghoff

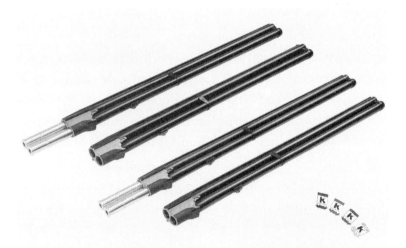

Skeet guns with carrier barrels allow sub-gauge tubes to be utilized. Competitors can use the same gun with similar to identical handling and balance in all four gauges. Photo courtesy of Krieghoff

The gun should never be held tightly. Braun suggested that the shooter hold the forend as if he were holding four or five eggs.

There are many excellent books on skeet shooting and a tiny one by Braun, *Skeet Shooting with D. Lee Braun*, is about as good as any. Certainly, he was the professional shot of his day. In his books and others you will find detailed lists of leads from each house. While they are useful tools and certainly correct in terms of relative perception from station to station, they really can only be guidelines. If you shoot maintained lead as opposed to swing through the perception of distance will vary dramatically. In other words, you must discover the lead and the sight picture that works for you. Then memorize it. Remember what it looked like, what it felt like.

When you finally break a target you find difficult, close your eyes and replay the shot in your mind. Remember where you first saw it, what your hold point was, and the speed with which you moved the gun. Then just keep doing it the same way. Realize that if you shoot the bird at different places on its path, the lead and the sight picture will change.

I often practice sporting clays on the skeet field, shooting doubles in reverse order. While it is great practice for sporting clays, it will not make you a top competitive skeet shot. If that is your goal, then you must strive for perfection and this can only be achieved by consistency, which includes a consistent break point. To learn leads, either as a new shooter or as someone who wants to improve his or her game, I seriously suggest practicing just one or two stations instead of shooting an entire round if your gun club will allow it. Just like a tennis player who uses a ball ma-chine to hone his swing, you can ingrain in your mind and in your muscle memory one or two stations.

When I teach beginners on the skeet field I normally like to start with a straightforward incomer, usually station one or seven depending on the wind and the sun. I don't want to start with station seven low house, as that teaches the beginner to shoot a static gun, or at least one with minimal movement and no follow through. I want the shooter to understand that there is a lead and that gun movement and follow through are key. Once they can break five or ten straight targets I move to the next and again shoot the incomer. When this is learned, I proceed to the other side of the field so that they get the idea of swinging from both sides. This is generally enough for the first day.

In an ideal world, I would start the shooter off the same way the second day. Each time he shows consistency, we would change stations. When he can break all four incomers from houses one, two, six, and seven, I would start him on crossing and going-away targets. Here I actually prefer to start with station four. Although it does have a long perceived lead, I find a crossing shot more straightforward than a quartering bird. After the shooter learns to handle high four by shooting a few birds a row, we proceed to the low house. If they have a good feel for station four, they have had a good day. The third day would be a review of the previous day's work and, if the shooter is up to it, going-away birds from two, three, five, and six would be added. The fourth day it would be doubles followed by high one and low seven and by the high and low shots at station eight.

The shooter who takes this approach to learning skeet will advance much more rapidly than the shooter who merely shoots round after round without discipline or without being able to spend time memorizing the sight picture for each station.

There has been a trend, especially in trap and international trap, toward light loads at very high velocity. These hypervelocity target loads work well on birds that are going away or traveling at a shallow angle. This is because these loads reach the target a few feet sooner. This can mean the difference between shooting at a bird that is still rising or blowing over a target that has begun to drop. On crossing birds, clays or game, it makes much less difference because there are very few inches saved in lead. In this situation, it's probably not worth the greater recoil or the increased number of pellets deformed at the base of the wad when shooting hypervelocity 1⅛-ounce or 1¼-ounce loads.

THE STATIONS

Station One, High and Low. High one is very straightforward. Starting at the center stake, bring the gun up to about a 30-degree angle (to the height of the target.) Bring your eyes halfway back to the house to look for the bird, call "Pull" as soon as you're under the bird and see a little bit of air, fire, and follow through.

For low one, start at the stake and bring your gun two-thirds of the way back to the house. Bring your eyes halfway back from your gun to the house and break it close to the stake. If you're shooting a gun with a cylinder choke, at twenty to twenty-five yards your effective pattern should have about a thirty-inch diameter. If you wait for the target to be ten yards from you, your pattern is only about twenty inches, but shoot it the way you prefer. Practice shooting this bird at the point where you will break it for doubles.

Station Two, High and Low. Although I shoot almost all of my targets with a maintained lead, I shoot high two and low six with an accelerating gun, more pull away than maintained. (As I never let the bird beat my barrel, swing through doesn't enter the equation.) Most shooters will see about a two-foot lead. When you see the lead, memorize it.

Low two is an easy bird, with the same routine as above. In other words, start at the stake, go two-thirds of the way back to the house (give or take), look halfway between your hold point and the house, then break the target where you will break it in doubles.

Stations Three, Four, and Five—High. According to Braun, the correct lead on all of these is the same; a bit more than three feet will suffice. Nevertheless, he recommends seeing 4 to 4½ feet of lead. In that fashion, if you happen to check your bead and slow the gun you still have a little extra margin of error. (There is much more margin of error to the front due to the length of the shot string.) Now this is really important: As soon as the lead looks right, fire and follow through. It *never* gets better. This doesn't mean that you can't spend a nanosecond double-checking your sight picture. It just means that if it looks good, shoot. Trying to make a shotgun sight picture look exactly perfect, too accurate, makes you hesitant. This hesitation normally leads to focusing on the bead, stopping the gun, and missing behind.

Braun felt that high three and low five are the two toughest stations on the field for left- and right-handed shooters, respectively. Personally, neither of those has given me the slightest bit of trouble. The high two and low six are my bugaboos. If I break station two, there is a 99-percent probability that I will go clear for the round. I improved my shooting on those two stations by shooting them a lot and memorizing the sight picture and timing that works for me.

I'm sorry I never met Lee Braun, as there are many questions I'd have liked to ask him. For one thing, it certainly appears from his book that he always shot an unmounted gun. I also start this way, as I find that a mounted gun gets in my way visually. Yet I doubt that there are any top competitive skeet shooters today who don't shoot with a premounted gun.

On high house stations three, four, and five, I mount on the center stake at the height the bird flies. I then move the gun two-thirds of the way back to the high house. My feet are lined up with my front foot pointing slightly to the right of the center stake. My front knee is bent, and 55 to 60 percent of my weight is on my front leg. When I move back to the house I coil myself like a spring, yet I try to remain relaxed, comfortable, and confident. After I dismount the gun, I direct my eyes halfway between the gun hold point and the trap mouth. Braun talks about looking right into the mouth, but I cannot see the bird there. Perhaps he was one of those individuals who excelled at sports because he had such extraordinary visual acuity. Wherever you first see the bird is where you should look for it. I try to break the bird within a foot or two of the center stake. Sometimes, in windy conditions or unusual lighting situations, I see the bird late and shoot it late. The important thing is to shoot when the lead looks right, not a moment before, not a moment after.

Stations Three, Four, and Five—Low. This is basically just the reverse of the high house, with a couple of caveats. My front foot is set up with the toe pointing a little bit to the left of the stake. It is important with all targets to start on their line or a little bit below. If you start too high it is easy for the barrel to obscure the target. This is more important on low birds, or at least more obvious.

As the sight picture on stations three, four, and five is basically the same, if you can break one of them you can break them all. However, these crossers are often subject to changes in wind, at least in regards to the perception of the shooter. It is therefore most important to practice the stations on as many fields as possible to get the feel for them under a variety of conditions. For example, a strong wind from the high to low house will cause the high target to drop. Conversely, the same wind will slow and force the low target to rise. Staying with the target and a good follow through are particularly important at these times.

Shooting targets from station four is an outstanding way to practice. It's also helpful for teaching the shooter to call his own shots. For example, if you see that you're breaking the target on its nose, you are shooting well and only the slightest modification needs to be taken to the sight picture. If, on the other hand, you're breaking the back of the target you know that you need to increase your lead by at least a foot. (In sporting clays, breaks on the top or bottom of the clay can also show you where you're shooting.)

According to Lee Braun, low five is the most often missed target in skeet shooting for the right-handed shooter. The perception is that the target is getting away from you from this angle, causing you to rush the target. Actually, you have plenty of time, so just remain focused and relaxed and break the bird. Good foot position is critical in the middle stations so that your body can move smoothly. Tension, and the concomitant muscle tightening, is the kiss of death. You might get away with it for a bird or two, but not if you need to shoot a hundred or more.

LEAD AS A FUNCTION OF ANGLE

Now I'm going to confuse the situation slightly. The sight picture and lead from station four will vary slightly with each shooter, depending on how fast they move the barrels and how they perceive distance. Let us take it as a given, however, that the correct lead is 3½ feet. The truth is that if the correct lead at 21 yards is 3½ feet for a crosser, it is the *actual* correct lead for all stations. But it is not the perceived or seen lead.

Now let's look at another example. Go to station seven and shoot a low bird going away. Between the time that you pull the trigger and when the pellets smash the bird, it has traveled 3½ feet (with the speed of the pellets and clay remaining, in relative terms, the same). Now step to station six and shoot the low target. While visually the correct sight picture is only, say, two feet here, the target has still traveled the 3½ feet between the time that you pull the trigger and when the pellets smash the bird. Part of this has to do with the side of the shot column intercepting the target. No doubt when I was in high school or college I knew enough about geometry, trigonometry, and calculus to set up a mathematical model to explain this phenomenon. In my dotage I do not possess the skills. In the real world of shooting, I'm not even sure that this concern should be addressed, yet on a theoretical level I believe it's illuminating.

Station Six, High and Low. High six is one of the easiest stations on the field. It seems to be coming toward you forever and you can pretty much shoot where you please. If I'm practicing for sporting clays I try to take it early, perhaps halfway to the center stake. (I will also practice shooting it very late as a dropper so I can force myself to get under the bird.) If I'm shooting competition I try to shoot it just before the stake. Many competitive shooters prefer to take it a third of the way from the stake to the low house, or where they will take it as a second bird on doubles. The perceived lead here is perhaps 2½ feet.

The low bird, on the other hand, can be quite tricky. Because it seems to be getting away from you so fast that there is a tendency to blow past it, realize you've gone too fast too far, stop the gun, and miss behind. A good way to overcome this is to move your hold point a few feet closer to the stake. That way you won't have the feeling of the gun moving overly fast. If you're a swing-through shooter, you just have to touch the bird, fire, and keep going. Otherwise, a foot or so should suffice.

Station Seven, High and Low. You're on the home stretch now and should never miss high seven once you're shooting competition seriously. High seven is just like high six, except with a bit less lead. The correct lead will differ depending on where you shoot the target, but I believe killing the bird before it has a chance to drop offers the most consistent results.

For low seven, you need to be comfortable swinging to the left. Start your barrel low and on line with the target perhaps six to ten feet out from the mouth of the trap. Look into the trap house and again blend your barrel to the bird. Follow through will break this target. Low seven is the easiest shot on the field, but never take any shot for granted. I've done so, and I've missed. Just shoot the damn thing and make sure you do so before it drops and becomes tricky.

Station Eight, High and Low. A beginner feels that this is a difficult shot because it is so quick. In fact, it is one of the easier targets on the field. The key is to not let the bird beat your barrel and, as always, follow through. In both high and low birds, all you need to do is bring the tip of your barrel to the bird, fire, and finish. Some shooters like to blot the bird out. However, as a two-eyed shooter (i.e., shooting with both eyes open and focused on the target) I see the bird all the time. If I were a one-eyed shooter or shooting a side-by-side perhaps it would indeed disappear.

My foot position is the same as Lee Braun's. Sometimes I shoot it as he suggests, which is also the way I shoot partridge. Other times, I shoot as a sideways shot, maintaining the same foot position. In any case, start your gun along the path that the target will travel. (If you're a new shooter, watch the shooter ahead of you so that you can see what that line is.) Look right at the mouth of the trap house and as you see the target emerge bring the tip of the barrel to the bird. As soon as you feel that you are accelerating

Shooting a sporting clay "grouse butt": Note alternate grip of the leading, left hand with the index finger pointing in the direction of the target.

past the bird, fire and follow through. No perceived lead is necessary here.

TRAP

If there's an aspect of shotgunning sport with which I have not come to terms, it is definitely trap, or as the similar game is known in the U.K., DTL (Down the Line). On a good day at skeet I will shoot a ninety-eight or a ninety-nine gun down. At trap I've shot twenty-five straight, but it certainly doesn't occur regularly. For me, anything over ninety is a good score. Some days I am content, or have to be, with eighty-five.

To be honest, I rarely shoot a properly set up trap gun. Though I've owned them, they never improved my scores enough for me to stick with them. I have at least one fault, and perhaps two. First, I'm just not comfortable shooting gun up. Second, and probably more serious, I find it a difficult game on which to concentrate. Yes, I know that I only need to concentrate from the moment I call for the bird to the moment it breaks, but at some point in a round I start dreaming of bird shooting, redheads, or world peace. Go figure.

Nevertheless, I did take a trap clinic with expert Kay Ohye that was hugely informative. If I had my heart set on becoming a top trap shooter, I would certainly go to several more of his clinics, or to those given by other top coaches, to enhance my knowledge. Still, I am analytical by nature and can provide a solid look at the basics of the sport. Some of the information provided below may overlap slightly with other sections of this chapter, but I think it's important to discuss each game completely.

As with every type of shooting, fundamentals are the key to trapshooting success. Start with your stance. You must be relaxed and balanced and be able to twist from the waist. If you pull back with your upper body as you shoot, you will shoot high. If you turn down and into the shot, you will shoot low. You should stand as erect as possible, with your leading foot slightly bent and your feet in a comfortable position from which you can twist left or right as necessary. Your neck, too, should be fairly high, with the plane of your face perpendicular to the rib of the barrels. Don't cant your face; your eyes should be as level as possible. And don't turn your face downward, as this will give you a false sight picture. Indeed, if you wear glasses, your prescription will not even be correct.

By the way, everything discussed here is geared toward the right-handed shooter. If you're a lefty, just reverse the positions.

A two-eyed shooter has great advantages in that he can see the birds under the barrels, which allows him to hold the gun higher. When you see the bird emerge from the trap, lock onto it with your eyes, go to it with the barrels, get to the far edge, fire, and follow through. This generally holds for sixteen-yard targets.

Some shooters, particularly those who move their barrels more slowly, will need to see some lead. But not much. The bird that gets away from you, especially at a more acute angle, will obviously need more lead. You need to shoot the bird while it is still rising. With a properly set up trap gun that shoots 60 or 70 percent high, you should be able to see the target as you fire. If your shotgun shoots flat—your game gun, for instance—you will have to power through the bird and it may be obscured as you fire.

Gunfit, although very different for trap than sporting clays, is still equally important. You must choose a gun that fits you well without being so heavy that it exhausts you nor so light as not to track well. This can only be determined by your own body size, shape, and strength.

Looking down the rib you should see the beads lined up one under the other. If one obscures the other, you probably have too much drop. If there's a significant gap between the beads you have too little drop. (This might be the correct sight picture for handicap if you shoot a gun with an adjustable comb.)

If the middle bead is to the left or right of the centerline as you look down the rib, the cast is wrong. A good way to determine this is to close your eyes, mount the gun as you normally would, and then open your eyes. What you see in this fashion is your true gunfit. Don't crane your neck, or face, or anything else to make the beads stack, as this "artificial" gunfit won't carry over into shooting. Remember, your eye is your rear sight; actually, it might be considered both sights.

For the trap shooter, length and weight of the barrels and weight and balance of the entire gun are very important. Your own strength and reflexes will determine which gun suits you best. The stronger you are, the faster your reflexes, the longer a barrel you can handle. In trapshooting one hundred birds is the minimum race, so you'll need to handle that gun comfortably for long stretches.

Since we're discussing barrels, we might touch on chokes here. The two go hand in glove. Different shooters have different choke requirements. Today, most trap guns are fitted with interchangeable choke tubes. This makes altering constriction a snap. Personally, a modified choke works well for me from the sixteen-yard line. I like the margin of error it gives me, along with a dense pattern. If you seriously want to improve your shooting, pattern your gun to determine whether it prefers Remington or Federal shells or some other brand. In all likelihood your barrel will handle some loads better than others. Even distribution is just as important as the total number of pellets. And don't forget to check for point of impact. If you become a true competitor, it is probably a good idea to do this with all the chokes you intend to shoot with at competition. While an onerous task, it should pay off with trophies.

By lengthening forcing cones and using over-bored barrels, you can produce denser, more even patterns. If you do change the bore diameters, just realize that this will also affect your choke tubes because the constriction is determined in relation to the barrel as it was originally set up. Also, be careful not to take out so much metal when back-boring that your wall thickness is below the manufacturer's recommended guidelines. As you step farther back toward the twenty-seven-yard line, you will of course need to increase the choke to improved modified (three-quarter choke) and then full with increased yardage.

Most trap guns have a stock that is shorter than on a game or sporting clay gun; as the barrel heads to vertical on an overhead target the thumb comes back toward the nose. All I can suggest here is to experiment or use the services of a qualified gunfitter who understands this game.

There is another aspect related to length of pull that must be addressed—climate. This may not matter much for shooters in Florida or California, but it certainly will for anyone who shoots in seasons that differ dramatically. There is at least ¼ inch of difference between the thickness of a light summer vest and a winter shooting coat. Pachmayr used to manufacture a wonderful interchangeable pad system, where pads of different lengths could be easily slipped on and off, but they shelved it.

Drop at comb and cast at the face are perhaps the two most important dimensions for trap shooters. Today, many companies supply trap stocks with adjustable combs. This is very useful, as it allows the competitive shooter to get a custom fit yet still change point of impact by raising the comb if shooting handicap events.

Again, good gunfit is related to a good gun mount. If you don't have a consistent gun mount, even the best gunfitter in the world won't come up with the correct dimensions. Because the trap shooter starts with a premounted gun, a good gun mount and gunfit are a little bit easier to accomplish. Just remember to always place the gun in the same pocket of your shoulder and at the same height, and maintain proper head placement without—or with minimal—canting to the side or tilting forward. (For more details on gun mount, please refer back to the section on skeet.)

Keeping the mounting process as comfortable and relaxed as possible is just as important for the trap shooter as the skeet shooter. Too much tension will exhaust you and prevent you from turning in your best possible performance. If you do get a bad mount, instead of trying to adjust it in the gun-up position, dismount and remount the gun. Similarly, if you get a "no bird," dismount and start your process all over again. This will conserve energy and preserve focus.

The next element to master is what Ohye calls "line shooting." The two worst things a shooter can do are spot shooting a target or waiting until the target drops. Each target that leaves the trap flies on a unique line. The shooter needs to intersect this line and travel with it for a distance to establish the correct line. If you follow the flight path starting from a point below its arc you pretty much eliminate the need to worry about elevation when you fire. Don't waste time by going to the point where the bird left the house and then following the exact line. Instead, intersect it and then travel with the target to establish this line.

As with all shooting, you should start on a line below that of the target so that your barrels don't obscure your vision. By doing this in trap, you are also creating the correct momentum upward to break the bird. You should start moving the gun as soon as the bird appears in your peripheral vision. Don't wait until you have a hard focus on the bird, as that will make you slow. You should always strive to break the target while it is rising, as this is when its path is most predictable, which leads to more consistent success. If you wait for it to flatten out it will probably be dropping by the time the shot arrives, and you will shoot over the bird. Hyper-fast light loads are very successful in international trap because they get to the target a few feet sooner, before it has a chance to drop.

The last aspect of actually shooting the target is follow through, or finish. Keep in mind that the shot is not complete until the pellets have actually left the barrel. Always finishing your shots will give you much more control of your gun. This is especially important on birds caught by the wind or when shooting in difficult conditions or from handicap yardage. Avoid starting to dismount or slowing your swing too soon.

Let's assume that you've been practicing your gun mount, that your gun fits you, that the gun shoots to the correct point of impact, that you keep your head still and in the right place, and that you turn laterally from the waist. Now it's time to shoot.

I'm a big believer in "correct" practice. This involves more than just going out and shooting rounds. It means that you are shooting clays in a manner that will allow you to shoot them more consistently. Practice until the shot becomes ingrained, an act of muscle memory. The best way to accomplish this is to throw a predictable clay, one that isn't oscillating randomly from right to left. This usually involves getting to know someone at your local trap range, as you'll need to have the machine set up to throw a fixed target. If you can get four friends to practice with you, it might be easier to get the field to yourselves.

Set the trap machine so it throws clays directly away from station three; in other words, straightaway shots. Set your feet as you need them, make sure your mount is perfect, go to your hold point (if you are a two-eyed shooter look under your barrels), and call for the bird. You know exactly where it is going so you should be able to break it every time. Memorize the shot. When you're breaking birds consistently, go on to the next station. Keep on until you've finished all five stations.

Now shoot a complete round, but don't change the trap machine. If you feel that you're shooting well, it is time to proceed.

This time, set the machine to throw an extreme right angle bird. Shoot it from station one. Here it is just a going-away target. As you move farther to the right, both the acuteness of the angle and the required lead increase. After you shoot all five positions well, shoot a complete round, but again do not change the trap machine. If you're happy with your shooting it is again time to move on.

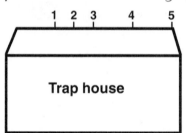

The one-eyed shooter should generally hold at the front edge of the trap house with the numbers 1–5 referring to the shooter's position on the field. A two-eyed shooter can hold higher, say eighteen inches or so, because he will see the bird below his barrels if he takes a 'soft' focus. Wind and other considerations affect exact hold point.

This time set the machine to throw a target to the extreme left. Begin this routine on station five, the easiest target. Once you're breaking birds consistently, move from right to left—five to four to three to two to one. Station one will give you the most acute angle. When you're shooting all five stations well, shoot a complete round, but again do not change the trap machine. This is what I call productive practice. (Obviously the trap can be set to throw intermediate angles for practice, as well.)

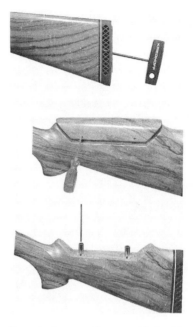

You've probably broken a lot of targets by now. We don't want to exhaust you. Fatigue leads to poor results, so if you have already shot a couple of hundred targets don't shoot an entire round at this point. Go home. Read a book, play tennis, go for a walk. Let your mind digest all of this. You will be a better shooter for it.

Trap stocks are often provided with combs that are adjustable for drop and cast. They are available from many manufacturers and in the aftermarket. Photo courtesy of Krieghoff

HANDICAP TARGETS

Handicap targets have three main components: short handicap, medium, and long. Short handicap refers to targets out to twenty-two or twenty-three yards; long out to twenty-six or twenty-seven yards. Short handicap targets are not much different than sixteen-yard targets, and the fundamentals you established while learning this game should carry over. In your practice sessions, again using a trap with a locked arm, make certain that you're shooting well at the seventeen-yard line before moving back to the eighteen and so on. As you move back there will be a psychological barrier that must be surmounted.

Although sustained lead may have worked well at the short yardage, you may find it easier to shoot longer targets with more of a swing-through or pull-away style. For one thing, the faster you're moving the barrels, the less perceived lead you will need to see. For another, it is common for maintained-lead shooters to slow or stop their guns at long handicap yardage. You must practice handicap targets on a regular basis to maintain form. Without practice, consistent execution won't be there. If at any time your form breaks down or your results suffer, go back to basics at shorter yardages. When you're happy at the shorter yardage, step back.

DOUBLES

The key to successful doubles is to shoot the first target quickly; in fact, as fast as you can. This should enable you to take the second target before it starts to descend. A falling target at trap is difficult. Since you already know the flight of the bird, you should know where to look for the target and be able to jump all over it. As Kay Ohye told me, it makes more sense to be a little reckless on the first target and to break all the second targets. In his small but excellent book, *You and the Target,* he writes, "If you miss two first targets and break all the second targets, you'll end up with a score of ninety-eight. If you use the break-all-the-first-targets theory, you may miss ten second targets and end up with a ninety. I would take the ninety-eight—how about you?"

As soon as you have broken the first target, move quickly to the second. Since you know its flight path, let your eyes shift to it and the gun will follow. Focus on the target well before your barrel reaches it or you'll never attain consistency.

While there is certainly an element of individual style, I recommend taking the right target first on stations one, two, and three and the left target first on stations four and five. As a right-handed, two-eyed shooter, I think this combination is the quickest. And, after all, doubles is largely about shooting quickly.

TRIGGERS AND FLINCHES

The worst thing that can happen to a shooter's confidence is to develop a flinch. It tends to be caused by one of two issues, and sometimes both. The first issue is just the pounding that one takes while shooting. Shooting a heavy load hundreds of times is like standing still while someone beats on your shoulder again and again. Throw in the barrel flip, which after a long day can cause quite an ache against your cheek or neck, and a flinch might just be in your future.

The best way to deal with a flinch is to not develop one. It is more easily prevented than cured. Part of the equation lies in knowing your own physical limitations. For example, some shooters never develop a flinch from shooting normal (1⅛ ounce) trap loads from an over-under, while others might develop one while shooting a light one-ounce load in an autoloader. I've seen all sorts of flinches—sometimes the shooter steps forward, sometimes he seems to push the gun, sometimes he seems to pull the gun.

Let's look at some basic principles for avoiding flinch. Light loads recoil less than heavy loads, and a heavier gun generates less recoil. This is certainly true, yet the cartridges from some manufacturers do seem to be more pleasant to shoot than others, even when they produce the same exterior ballistics. Autoloaders absorb more recoil than a fixed-breech gun and some types of autoloader are more pleasant to shoot than others. Gas-operated systems such as the Beretta or Remington seem to do the best job at creating a mild shove (as opposed to the hard push of a fixed-breech gun). While trap and wildfowling are primarily 12-gauge sports, 20- and 28-gauges can be used effectively in practice sessions at skeet or sporting clays, for most game shooting situations, and, obviously, in gauge-specific competitions.

All guns can be made to shoot more pleasantly in a few different ways. The easiest way is to add a recoil pad that does a good job of absorbing shock; again, some brands are better than others. A more labor intensive and expensive method is to lengthen the forcing cones and back-bore the barrels. Porting, which forces gases upward, reduces muzzle flip, which in turn allows the shooter to get on the next target faster and eases the jolt to the neck over the long term. Adding weight to the butt stock or the barrels, or preferably both, helps keep the balance point where you want it while slightly reducing felt recoil. There are even stocks on the market designed on a hydraulic system that absorbs even more recoil.

In my old age, I find that a gel pad inserted into my vest does a great job at making a long shooting day more comfortable. I prefer the soft versions. The drawback, of course, is that if you wear one consistently you will slightly alter your length of pull.

A bad trigger may also create a flinch. The worst triggers have a significant amount of slack and/or a significant amount of creep. Both destroy your timing. Most competitive shooters require a trigger pull of about three pounds, completely devoid of creep or slack. It is easier to adjust to a heavier trigger pull than it is to deal with creep or slack.

When you pull the trigger you disengage the sear, which allows the hammer to fall. Some shooters develop a flinch by lightening their trigger so much that on some unconscious level they become afraid of touching it for fear of a premature discharge. (No need to call Dr. Freud, just go to a trigger expert—less expensive, more rewarding.)

If you develop a flinch and can't cure it through normal means, as described above, there is another alternative—the use of a release trigger. Release triggers are not for the beginner, the uncommitted, or the absent minded because you pull the trigger, call for the bird, and release the trigger to disengage the sear.

More than one trap house has been shot by someone whose mind wandered while holding down the trigger. Release triggers are pretty much limited to the trap field.

Some serious trap shooters develop a flinch on only the first shot of doubles, but it doesn't seem to enter into other parts of their game. Some of these gents have overcome the problem by using a release/pull-trigger system. In other words, the trigger releases on the first shot and is pulled normally on the second. If you do go to a release trigger, make sure that it is installed by a manufacturer with a good reputation, warranty, and design. I recommend that you don't tinker with this trigger at all. If it needs work, return it to whoever installed it unless you're absolutely certain that your gunsmith can handle the job.

I suppose this is as good a spot as any to go into "lock time." This is the time between when you pull the trigger and when the firing pin is struck by the falling hammer. Theoretically, the faster this time is, the less follow through you'll need. Some guns are much quicker than others, but as long as your gun isn't too terribly slow it won't matter much. There is one caveat, though. Let's say, for example, that you shoot an old autoloader with a slow lock time on your normal trap shots and handicap targets but an over-under with much faster lock times for doubles. This difference between guns may affect your timing. If your favorite autoloader has a particularly slow lock time, you may be able to purchase a kit that will speed it up. Your goal should always be to make as many things as possible consistent in your shooting.

SPORTING CLAYS

Finally we come to sporting clays, the shooting game about which I know the most. It's a game that I can sink my teeth into, at least if it has the right sauce.

In addition to having shot a lot of clays, I've taken at least a few lessons from some of the top men in the business, including A. J. "Smoker" Smith, Mickey Rouse, Michael Rose, Gary Herman, and Keith Lupton. I've also been lucky enough to have theoretical discussions with a number of other top men like Chris Batha and Ed Anderson.

I've even taken a lesson here and there with a couple of the guys from Holland & Holland, specifically Ken Davies and Rex Gage. Although they are good men for teaching beginners the fundamentals of game shooting, I found their techniques of marginal use for serious sporting clays or really difficult tall driven birds.

This gun mount is too low. The head is forced down and everything is tight and strained. Bring the gun to your face, not your face to the gun. Photo courtesy of Renata Coleman

Many of the basic principles that apply to sporting clays have been addressed elsewhere, but they are so vital that I will cover them here step-by-step.

Because sporting clays is a gun-down discipline, and because the targets are so difficult and demanding these days, nothing less than a correct gun mount will suffice. So let's again start with the stance. You need to be erect, balanced with your weight slightly forward, and relaxed, with your leading toe pointing toward the break point of the target. As you will be shooting two birds at each station, it is possible that your foot position will be a compromise between the two targets or, in some circumstances, oriented for the more difficult shot. Your stance should be fairly narrow, with your feet no wider than your shoulders, and probably closer than that.

The gun will be coming across your body at about a 45-degree angle, making contact with the natural pocket formed just inside the shoulder. The heel of the butt plate should settle at about the top of your shoulder. The

This is much better, but with a borrowed gun I'm tilting my head a bit more than I would like, and from this angle my thumb seems a little close to my nose—indicative of a stock that is too short. Photo courtesy of Renata Coleman

gun should reach your face and shoulder simultaneously, or at least close to it. The plane of your face should be perpendicular to the rib. Don't cant your face or tilt it more than minimally forward. Your neck should be slightly forward but not enough to cause neck strain; eyes should remain as level as possible.

When shooting sporting clays you should always "think out the station to make the shot as easy as possible." Smoker Smith told me that, and he was right. Sometimes it can be as simple as moving to the left or right of the station rather than standing in the middle. Sometimes it means breaking the first target at a spot where picking up the second target will be easier. For example, in some cases you might want to take the first bird later than

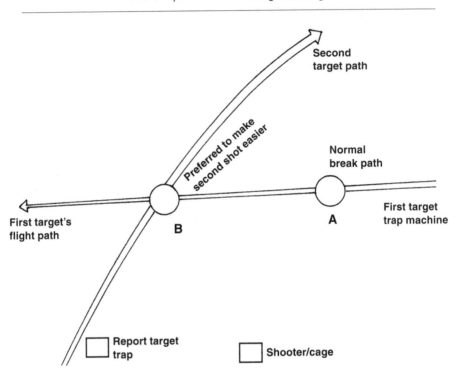

Thinking out the station: Presume A is the ideal normal break point for the first target. However, with this report pair, one is better off shooting it at B to be in an ideal position for the second target and eliminating the need to rush after the first shot to chase the second target.

usual. Envision a report pair: the first a crosser from right to left and the second a bird to the right that is initially visible where you broke the first bird—if you took it late. If the first bird had been shot in the normal fashion, the second would have traveled quite a distance before you could pick it up.

SIGHT POINT

This is the point at which you first see the target. Watch the competitors shooting before you and observe the flight of the target. Take note of the point where the bird starts to drop because it is slowing (you generally want to break it before it drops), and look for any curve in the clay's path. By tilting the trap to the left or right and using other tricks the course designer can add interesting variations to the target's trajectory. Get a feel for where you first see the target and where you want to lock onto it.

For example, you might be able to spot the target coming off the trap arm but that may not be where you want to cast your gaze. You don't want to see the bird, or least you don't want to concentrate on the bird, before the spot where you will start your mount. You just want a soft focus in the area. As you pick up the bird, lock onto it with your eyes. (As a great Italian live pigeon shot once said to me, "The eyes go to the bird and the hands follow.") Your gun mount should be sure and deliberate, not forced or tense. Your gun needs to be closer to the break point because the eyes are faster than the hands. This brings us to the hold point.

HOLD POINT

Start your gun barrels between your sight point and your break point. This gives you time to move the gun toward the target and blend the tip of the barrels to the bird. It has often been written that the hold point should be a third of the way between the sight point and the break point. In general this is good advice, but every bird is different, and in some cases the correct hold point might be just 20 percent and in others halfway to the target. This is something you can only learn through one-on-one tutelage or by experience.

I have wracked my brain to come up with an example where a shooter would start the barrels where he is looking, but I just can't do it. Even on a going-away bird like a station seven low at skeet, I like to carry my barrels a little bit below and to the side of the target in case it doesn't follow exactly the same path. Remember, never start your barrels above the line of the bird because that will obscure the target. The exact hold point will be determined by a number of factors, including your own reflexes and whether you shoot pull away or maintained lead.

BREAK POINT

Obviously, the break point is the spot where you want to smash your target. (You insert your barrels just before the break point.) Lots of factors are at play here. In normal circumstances, you should shoot the target where it is easiest to hit. The sole exception to this was discussed above, when you create a later break point that allows the second target to be picked up most efficiently. In general, you should break the target before it has a chance to drop. Once its trajectory drops you must remember to shoot under the bird, and a slowing, dropping target is more affected by the wind.

When you determine your break point, be aware of what the target is actually doing. If it's a quartering target set by a tricky course designer so that it curves away from you near the break point it will require less lead than if it traveled on a straight line.

CHOKES, LOADS, AND TARGETS

These three must always be taken together. Let's begin with the clays themselves as this is probably the most overlooked aspect of the game. The two most important concerns are surface area and the hardness/fragility of each type of clay. For example, a standard 110mm clay has about 3½ inches of surface area when seen from the side as presented in skeet, but over fourteen inches if viewed from the top or bottom. This is a significant difference and a much less dense load is required to break the target. View this another way: Cylinder or skeet chokes and No. 8s will break a high tower clay shot at forty-five yards (the bottom is the most fragile part of a clay target), whereas the same clay seen from the side will need at least a modified or full choke and a load of No. 7½s. Only on the rarest of occasions will a single pellet produce a visible piece, let alone a break.

Battues present almost no surface area when seen from the side, but wait for them to turn and a large easily breakable surface area presents itself. Just like shooting a high tower, you can use very little choke and a smaller pellet to break the target (the smaller the pellet, the greater the number in the load, the greater the density). The drawback with small pellets is that they lose energy quickly—and they don't have much to begin with. Twenty-five yards is about the maximum for No. 9s, even for targets taken from below.

Rabbits are physically a very hard target, but there is a caveat here. They are hard when taken edge-on. (Notice how well they bounce along the ground without breaking.) But like all targets they have a relatively fragile area, in this case a side-on presentation. Except for very long rabbits, if you can see the side No. 8s will do the trick. And at ten or fifteen yards, No. 9s will demolish a rabbit taken from the side. On the other hand, if you're placed on a cage above a rabbit station and the rabbit is going away from you edge-on, this is the time to go to No. 7½s.

Skeet or cylinder chokes are perfect for side-on targets out to about twenty-five yards. If you pattern your gun at thirty and thirty-five yards you will see that the area outside the center core becomes very thin. This is the point at which you need to change over to improved cylinder (quarter choke). For argument's sake, let's say that twenty-five yards is the maximum distance where you have sufficient density in your gun with a cylinder or skeet choke to consistently break standard targets. Now let's assume for a moment that instead of the standard target you are given a 90mm midi. You need to crank from cylinder to improved cylinder. This will ensure enough density.

Number 9s were marginally okay at twenty-five yards, but let's move the target back another five yards to thirty. Improved cylinder is still fine, but No. 9s have dropped off in energy. Go to No. 8s at thirty yards—and it's fine if you prefer them at twenty-five yards. If your target at thirty yards turns out to be a 60mm mini, improved cylinder is now marginal depending on how your gun patterns. (If your gun has been over-bored and your forcing cones lengthened you're more likely to have a dense enough pattern.) At this point it may be best to change to a modified choke (half choke in British nomenclature). And at thirty-five yards modified and No. 8s are definitely the way to go.

A target is most fragile from the bottom and toughest on the dome side of the outer edge. A number of sporting clays courses provide targets called "chukar valley" or something along those lines. On these shots, the shooter is often placed on a bridge or a pier so that the target appears from below, usually as a quartering shot. Although this offers you a large surface area at which to shoot, you will probably need improved cylinder and No. 8s. Whereas from the bottom, cylinder and No. 9s might have done the trick. (On a longer shot, you would probably need to bump up to modified and No. 7½s. The rule of thumb for each longer, tougher shot is to go one choke tighter and one shot larger.)

Kenneth Eyster is the American guru of barrel work. About twenty years ago I sent him a Model K-80, light version, and then he sent the barrels to Briley to have long choke tubes installed. He lengthened the forcing cones and back-bored the barrels. All tubes were originally the tightest they made, super full. He then hand honed each choke. The chokes were barrel specific and came in three configurations. Number one was a cylinder-like choke. It opened very quickly yet provided dense, even patterns. Number two was closest to modified but useful even on crossers out to almost forty-five yards, which is farther out than you would expect a modified barrel to perform well. Number three was a super full choke that literally smoked targets at well over fifty yards. It was truly amazing.

By hand honing each choke to a specific barrel (over or under) and linking it to a specific load—for example, Federal or Remington—Eyster created great efficiency. In addition to working out specific loads for clays, he also found the best flyer configurations.

My scores at skeet and sporting clays improved dramatically because of his work. Many top competition shooters like Andy Duffy had custom choke work done by Ken Eyster. I moved to Europe in 1996 and basically replaced sporting clay shooting with driven game. I was shooting so few targets that I sold the gun. What a fool. The gun shot like a dream, but I found it aesthetically lacking. I just didn't like the way it looked with its light-colored alloyed receiver and high gloss polyurethane finish. In retrospect, I should have had the stock refinished and lived with it. Now that I'm shooting clays again, I heartily miss that shotgun.

Gun	Barrel	Shell	Height	Distance	Coverage	Efficiency	Yield
Make, Model, S.N.	*Length Position Tube*	*Make & Load*					
K-80 13481							
Eyster SC #1		2¾–1⅛-8RL	+1	21	31.40	83.43	100
Over							
Eyster SC #3		3¼–1¼-8SP	−1	35	25.35	92.97	100
Over		3¼–1¼-8SF	−1.5	35	29.83	86.72	100
	Flyers 2nd shot						
Under							
Eyster SC #1		2¾–1⅛-8RC	0	21	31.65	84.80	100
Eyster SC #2		3¼–1¼-8SP	+1.5	35	29.23	85.35	100
	Flyers 1st shot	3¼–1¼-8SF	+1.5	35	29.84	80.47	100

Notes: The RL Rem will shoot a little tighter than regular 2¾-1⅛-8 Rem.
The SP (Win Super Pigeon) is better in these barrels than the SF (Fed Super Field).
Height is inches from top of front bead to center of impact.
Distance is in yards.
Coverage is in inches of diameter.
Efficiency is the percentage of total shot in a thirty inch circle.
Yield is the percentage of total shot on a field forty-eight x forty-eight inches.

This chart shows diameter of pattern with different chokes at appropriate yardage and how efficient patterns can be created through hand honing and cartridge selection.

Gun	Barrel	Shell	Height	Distance	Coverage	Efficiency	Yield
Make, Model, S.N.		Length	Make & Load				
		Position					
		Tube					
Back-bore, Competition Choke, Part, Briley Ext. Tubes							
Krieghoff K-80 13481 Barrels 13481							
13481	Over	2¾–1⅛-9 Rem	+0.7	15	27.98	95.02	100
	Eyster SC #1	2¾–1⅛-9 Rem	+0.2	21	32.69	81.00	100
		2¾–1⅛-8 Rem	−0.6	25	28.56	76.41	100
		2¾–1⅛-8 R/L	+1.6	30	29.66	56.06	90.04
Over	Over	2¾–1⅛-8 Rem	-0-	25	27.31	96.75	100
	Eyster SC #2	2¾–1⅛-8 Rem	−0.4	30	27.13	93.94	100
		2¾–1⅛-8 Rem	−0.4	35	28.56	83.12	100
	Over	2¾–1⅛-8 Rem	+1.0	35	25.75	93.07	100
	Eyster SC #3	2¾–1⅛-8 RL	+0.5	35	25.29	94.16	100
		2¾–1⅛-7½ RL	+0.6	35	24.94	94.85	100
Under	Under	2¾–1⅛-9 Rem	-0-	15	28.14	96.10	100
	Eyster SC #1	2¾–1⅛-9 Rem	-0-	21	32.88	81.46	100
		2¾–1⅛-8 Rem	-0-	25	28.20	71.00	100
		2¾–1⅛-8 R/L	+21.2	30	29.68	61.45	91.99
	Under	2¾–1⅛-8 Rem	-0-	25	25.96	97.40	100
	Eyster SC #2	2¾–1⅛-8 Rem	-0-	30	29.13	92.60	100
		2¾–1⅛-8 Rem	+1.2	35	29.11	85.50	100
	Under	2¾–1⅛-8 Rem	+1.0	35	26.05	92.49	100
	Eyster SC #3	2¾–1⅛-8 RL	-0-	35	25.69	93.95	100
		2¾–1⅛-7½ RL	+0.5	35	25.25	94.19	100

Height is inches from top of front bead to center of impact.
Distance is in yards.
Coverage is in inches of diameter.
Efficiency is the percentage of total shot in a thirty inch circle.
Yield is the percentage of total shot on a field forty-eight x forty-eight inches.
Over refers to top barrel and under refers to bottom barrel.

Hand honing allows the point of impact for each barrel to be moved slightly. Different loads provide different results. The needs of the clay target shooter are different from those who shoot boxed birds.

If you look at the chart you will see that at twenty-one yards the pattern extended to roughly 31½ inches and that about 84 percent of the pellets could be found within this span, depending on the barrel. No bird, not even a mini taken from the side, would fly through that pattern. This was also an ideal first shot on hand-thrown Columbaire targets. Eyster number two, the barrel of choice on boxed pigeon for the first shot, had a pattern of almost thirty inches, with over 80 percent of the pellets in the circle. For the second barrel, the top barrel, using No. 3s, there was a load-based choice of spread and efficiency: There was nearly 87 percent efficiency in thirty inches with Federal and a whopping 93 percent with Winchester at thirty-five yards.

Flyers, by the way, is a euphemism for live pigeon shoots. Boxed birds were the forerunners to trap; indeed, the term "trap" came from the sport and old lithographs depict gunners at English clubs shooting at pigeons being manually released from a

Boxed pigeons, also known as flyers, are an addictive target sport. Early versions were the forerunner to trap.

trap with a long cord. Today these shoots are still legal in a number of states, although normally competition is kept quiet, by invitation only. The bird must be retrieved within the ring and the shooter must fire both barrels, even at a bird killed with the first, to ensure that he does not shoot a bird boy retrieving a downed bird. In Columbaire, the thrower, like a baseball pitcher, tries to beat you. Betting is usually involved.

When patterning this gun Eyster soon came to the conclusion that it preferred Winchester to Federal flyer loads. This is something that can only be determined by actual experimentation. It should also be pointed out that by lengthening the forcing cones and back-boring the barrels Eyster created very dense patterns even without hand honing, but it is hand honing that produces the beautifully distributed, even patterns that reduce the likelihood of a target flying through and smoke the birds at long yardage. One of the reasons that the old English guns killed birds so well, and you must remember that cartridges were not nearly as good then, was because each gun was hand honed by a master for a specific load and for a specific use. Hand honing can also be used to change point of impact, within reason.

Cylinder choke in 12-gauge is generally defined as zero choke and skeet choke is generally defined as a barrel constriction of .005 or .006 (a.k.a. five or six points of choke). Improved cylinder is defined as .010, modified as .020, and full as .040.

Cylinder and skeet chokes are very similar, but if I had to choose just one it would be cylinder. Cylinder opens up a little bit sooner, and at the point where they are both dissipating it is time to go on to improved cylinder anyway. In fact, cylinder can have one, two, or three points of choke. That is when hand honing for a specific load really shines. I cannot think of a single instance when I would want more choke at less than twenty yards. To know how well your particular gun performs at twenty-five and thirty yards you're just going to have to go to a patterning plate. No need to count pellets; just look at it to determine where density is no longer sufficient.

At roughly thirty yards an improved cylinder choke covers perhaps ½ to 1½ inches more diameter than modified. In general, you could get along quite well with cylinder for close shots, modified for medium shots, and full for long targets. (Keep in mind that if you see the target from the bottom significantly less choke is required.)

All clays at sporting competitions are thrown as pairs. And in an ideal world each barrel would be choked for the particular target. This is fine if you're shooting a double-barrel shotgun. But what if you're shooting an autoloader? Let's say, for example, that you're being presented with a "fur and feather." The rabbit target is a close quartering target presentation, best shot at twenty yards or less. On report, a standard target is crossing at about thirty-five yards. If you had the choice you would shoot cylinder followed by modified. But you're shooting a single-barrel gun. What to do?

I would pop in an improved cylinder choke. For the first barrel I would shoot No. 9s, as they should open up quickly to give me nearly a skeet pattern. A faster load would be good, and I might even go to a felt wad, both of which would help open the pattern. For the second target, depending on my gun, I would go to a slightly slower No. 8 or perhaps a standard speed No. 7½. This would hold the pattern together longer.

In general, I think it is best to stick to one load, at least in regard to velocity. If you're used to a load that shoots at 1,350 feet per second (fps) and suddenly you're shooting cartridges at 1,100 fps you may well need a new sight picture. You definitely will if you go to a subsonic load. I recommend that you take a target load that your gun likes and that you can easily obtain. Use this load for the majority of your shooting. Shot size within these velocity parameters won't matter much as you are changing to larger, heavier pellets that retain velocity better as range increases anyway. Just change your cartridge speed when you need to effectively change choke performance in circumstances like those detailed above.

While shooting a single-barrel gun might seem a disadvantage, you may find that it actually improves your performance. The reason is simple: The gas-driven mechanism of an autoloader absorbs some of the recoil and spreads the period of time over which it is expended, thereby reducing felt recoil.

The key for sporting clays is to have your gun so well tuned that it is reliable. Proper cleaning is very helpful for this, as is having your gun tweaked slightly by a competent gunsmith. It is a good idea to have some trigger work done to remove any slack or creep in the trigger and to adjust the trigger pull according to your preference. Many companies are now doing aftermarket work on barrels, chokes, and triggers. And many of the manufacturers themselves are offering competition guns. For example, Beretta offers the new Teknys model that is adjustable for drop and cast at comb, and it comes with lengthened forcing cones, over-boring, and competition chokes. Most, if not all, of the work has already been done for you.

COURSE PRACTICE

Sporting clays has often been called golf with a shotgun. If I had a buck for every time a writer has used that as the lead, I could probably buy a decent bottle of single malt. There are similarities in that each course is distinct, both as a function of topography and the course designer's creative juices.

There are even a few courses where you can travel from station to station by golf cart. Casa de Campo in the Dominican Republic was the first shooting grounds I visited where this was standard operating procedure. This is one of the great sport-

ing clay fields of the world, created by the combined intelli-
gence of Jose Pepe Fanjul, the
owner and great wing shot, and
Michael Rose, one of the best instructors and gunfitters anywhere. Humewood Castle, my
own shoot in Ireland, and San-
danona in Millbrook, New York,
now owned by the Orvis Company, also employ carts.

I have often felt that because there is such a great variation of difficulty among the
different shooting grounds that
they should actually be rated.
Level one should be shooter

Special events are now offered for those who prefer to shoot side-by-side guns in sporting clays.

friendly, level two for intermediate shooters, level three for advanced and level four championship rank. While I do realize
that competitors shoot in their own classifications against shooters of roughly the same ability, a C or D competitor who is new
to the game is going to be quite disheartened if he shoots at a facility where long, deceptive birds are the rule.

The skeet field is actually a great place to get a feel for sporting clays. First of all, you can shoot the same target until you
know it so well that you can consistently break it. And it's cost efficient. Just remember to shoot with an unmounted gun and to
shoot the target as you would on a sporting clay field. If you're
shooting a field on your own or with a squad of like-minded
shooters there are many useful exercises that you can perform,
assuming you get the permission of the club and can alter the
normal way of shooting in a safe manner.

Here is a good example. Go to station four and shoot the targets as you normally would. When you're breaking them consistently, step back five yards. You will need more lead to connect, and when your brain has worked this out and memorized it, step back another five yards. Keep going as long as it remains safe for your trapper and the neighboring fields. When you get back to thirty yards you will need to switch from skeet or cylinder choke to improved cylinder and No. 8s. If you get close to forty yards, modified will take over. At forty-five, you'll probably want to switch to improved modified or full and No. 7½s.

This exercise will teach you many things. First, it should improve your ability to judge distance. This is very important for sporting clays because you can't make the right choke and cartridge choices unless you can judge the distance to the break point (unless you use a rangefinder). To help get a feel for distance, remember that it is twenty-one yards to the center stake from all stations, and that it is roughly forty yards from the high house to the low.

The next thing that you will learn is that as distance increases, so does lead. While this may sound obvious, there is a corollary: Lead is not perfectly linear. If it were, when you went from twenty to forty yards you could just double the lead. In reality, you will probably need to go two to four feet farther than double the lead. There is an obvious reason for this. The farther you are from your target, the more slowly your pellets are traveling when they reach the target. Also, the longer targets produce a smaller visual/barrel angle so there is an increased tendency to slow your swing. But the target's speed has not changed. Actually, it's slowing from the moment it leaves the arm, but when it's crossing the center stake it is traveling the same speed whether you're shooting from twenty yards or forty.

If you've shot both the high and low birds all the way back to forty yards, and have learned to shoot them well, you've had a good day and should probably call it quits. If you've shot on your own it was probably fairly tiring. But whether you shoot again on the same day or another, do try the same exercise from stations three and five. Move back on the same angle so that only the distance is changing. When you can break all of these three stations consistently at all yardage from twenty to forty you have really accomplished something. (This may take many days to achieve.) Pat yourself on the back, have a swig of Jack Daniel's, smoke a good cigar, and think of me. I'm suggesting that now, of course, because the next exercise is probably going to cause you to hate my guts.

Next, start by shooting station four at thirty yards. You will need improved cylinder choke and No. 8s. Start with the high bird and try and break it at different places. If you're breaking it successfully at the stake, try to hit it five feet sooner. Now try for ten feet sooner. At the point where you can no longer connect with the target (i.e., it is an unrealistic shot) return to shooting it over the stake. Now try taking it farther and farther away. As you make these changes you will need to change your foot position and your hold point. Learn to break the target as a dropping bird, which may require a modified choke.

Now switch to the low bird. Shoot exactly as described above for the high station. In shooting the station in this fashion you will have learned both to challenge the target and to handle dropping birds. You will also be getting an idea of your limitations. This is handy because it will show you how, and more importantly where and when, you should be handling similar sporting clay targets.

Here's where they get really difficult. Get the trapper to throw report pairs; first from the same house, then from opposite houses. Practice taking them in either order. When you can do this well enough, have him throw true pairs. When you start shooting these well, practice shooting them as you would in sporting clays; for example, shooting one bird early and the other late. This is really tricky. Don't expect to break all the birds, but when you feel that you're shooting them well move back another five yards, repeating everything you did from thirty yards. If you take your birds quite late, you may need to go to modified choke. In fact, it might even have made sense to do this at thirty yards. This is something only you can judge. If you're shooting a double-barrel gun you might want to consider shooting improved cylinder and modified on this station and at the previous yardage.

On separate days, go through this same program at stations three and five. Stations two and six would also be useful for practicing this exercise except that on most fields there is usually a divide between skeet layouts that prevents you from getting very far back.

As you work your way up the competitive ladder and find yourself shooting more difficult tournaments you may even want to try this exercise from forty yards and beyond. While it may seem tedious and difficult, it will pay dividends. A few days of this type of practice session is definitely helpful.

DEALING WITH TARGETS

If birds are coming at you (as a right-handed shooter) it is best to take the bird on the right first. Right-handed shooters have a tendency to take the gun away from the face as they move to the right and bring it toward the face (i.e., hold tight) on birds to the left. In general, it is better to take the low bird of a true pair first. This is because recoil will often bring you up toward the second shot, and if you shoot them in the reverse order the low bird is more likely to disappear before you can get a good shot at it. Ninety-five percent of the time I will shoot the first bird of a true pair and then go on to the second. On rare occasions, it makes sense to shoot the rear bird first and then go on to the lead target. You must be careful that the birds are not too close together from a visual perspective. In that case, the tendency is to shoot between them. This never works. In fact, course designers often throw birds that look like they can be broken with the same shot pattern. It rarely works out that way and you are more likely to shoot between the two targets and miss both. Take a hard focus on one, ignoring the second until after the first is broken.

Crossers

Crossers on sporting clays courses are likely to be long targets. They are also likely to be deceptive shots. Designers will often throw the birds using the curvature of the ground to give the appearance of flying flat, when they are actually dropping. At major shoots, it is not uncommon to see a bird that needs twelve to fourteen feet of lead and that must be shot under by two or three feet.

Choke selection is critical, as crossers present you only a small surface area. You must learn to judge distance accurately, and a rangefinder can be a very handy device. Reading off the target itself may or may not prove successful. It might be better to get a reading off a tree or rock in your break zone and adjust from there. (Only you and your rangefinder can determine how best to quickly make a yardage determination.) If you take the measurement from three paces behind the cage, subtract the appropriate yardage.

Rangefinders—such as this offered by Bushnell—allow sportsmen to quickly and accurately judge distances. Photo courtesy of Bushnell Performance Optics

Watch the way the target flies and try to determine where it is slowing and dropping. Depending on where it is most easily broken, you should either take it early before it drops or, if that is not practical, deal with it by shooting under the target.

Hitting long birds requires much more precision. Shooting cylinder choke at a twenty-yard target produces a thirty-inch pattern. This means that you can be fifteen inches over or under the bird and still break it. At thirty-five to forty-five yards you're probably shooting a pattern, at least a useful dense pattern, of only around twenty-five inches. Not only have you reduced the margin of error to twelve inches, you have done it over double the distance. In other words, the degree of angle that you can be off and still break the target is now less than half of what it was.

Quartering targets are by nature deceptive. A target at a very shallow angle looks like it needs no lead, but in reality this is only the case for straightaway birds. Unfortunately, these birds are also easily missed in front. If the angle is truly shallow and you shoot three feet to the side your pattern and the target may never intersect. Interestingly, quartering birds with a bit more angle, especially long quartering birds, may need quite a bit of lead, at least in terms of perception. This is something that you will only discover by shooting a lot of targets. Trigger time, memorizing leads, and the type of practice described earlier in this section will stand you in good stead at competitions.

Low incomers, often called Spanish partridge in sporting clay nomenclature, can be tricky for two reasons. First, as these are often in-your-face targets your pattern is quite small, even when shooting cylinder choke. You just don't have much margin of error. Second, pairs are often thrown so that you have to shoot the first bird very quickly to have a shot at the second bird. The best way to shoot these targets is to jump all over the first bird with maintained lead. As soon as the sight picture is good, really just when the gun hits your face, fire and follow through just enough to ensure a hit, then go aggressively to the second target. Right-handers will have a much easier time shooting the right bird first.

High Tower

If there is one target at which I excel, it is the high tower shot. It just feels natural for me. This may have something to do with the fact that I have been shooting tall driven pheasant for a long time now. When I was shooting clays a lot, I found it best to shoot this target with a maintained lead. If it were directly over-head, I would just pull in to the right position in front of it, fire, and follow through. Often I would actually see the bird float-ing below my barrels as a halftone. As I shoot much more game than clay targets these days, I find pull away works a little bit better for me now.

I have very few claims to fame in the clay target world, but two of the three occurred on high towers. On the first occasion, I was the only man to run the sta-tion out of 175 guns, which in-cluded Smoker Smith at the top of his game, John Kruger and Andy Duffy, and Gary Herman, who was the chief instructor for the U.S. Sporting Clays Asso-ciation at the time. The second

This gun is almost long enough to fit me when length of pull is measured, but not for overhead shot.

happened down at Casa de Campo, when I won the one-man flurry with a score of 37 out of 50; clays being thrown at all angles from all three heights of the tower. Casa de Campo, as part of Pepe Fanjul's Sugar Clay Invitational shoot, had both one-man and three-man flurries off the high tower. This is one of the best high towers in the world, the tallest at about 120 feet.

I'm not saying this to brag, but merely to reassure. When it comes to a high tower, I do know what I'm talking about.

High tower targets require a fair bit of reading. For example, how far away is the target when you shoot it? Also, for birds that aren't directly overhead, what is the target doing? Is it rising or is it dropping? The high tower at Casa de Campo was particularly tricky. The bird coming straight at the shooter was easy enough to deal with, although it did require quite a bit of lead. The bird going over the shoulder to the left was dropping, so if you were thinking of the hands of a clock, you would want to shoot at 7:30 or 8:00, not 9:00. The bird going off to the right was farther away and needed almost twice the lead as the bird to the left. Also, because of the way the trap arm was set, it was rising slightly, allowing you to shoot directly on the same line or just a hair high. (Of course it did drop but after optimal break zone.)

To complicate things even more, some days they would throw standard targets and other days midis. The midis flew faster, but because they were smaller, they also gave the impression of being farther away than they actually were.

As noted earlier, if you can see the bottom of the clay target, cylinder and skeet chokes coupled with No. 8s work well to forty or even forty-five yards. If the bird is not coming directly toward you, with the entire bottom obvious, I would change to improved cylinder. For a perfect incoming target, if you're a two-eyed shooter with an over-under or autoloader, you will probably see the bird as a halftone under your barrels. If you do, and you break a bird, this is the sight picture you should establish. If you don't see the target under your barrels when you break it, keep shooting in exactly the same way—same hold point, same break point, same barrel speed and timing.

If a midi is presented instead of the standard clay, I would probably change to improved cylinder to ensure a dense enough pattern on birds over thirty yards away. Minis thrown off high towers are great fun. If you're close to the trap the target will be moving at high speed and will require quite a bit of lead. In fact, this is one of my favorite targets for practicing for tall pheasant shoots. (The other is a battue, because when it's taken from the bottom it can be made to replicate a curling pheasant as it shifts in the breeze.)

To ensure a dense enough pattern for minis, you will either need to increase the amount of choke or go to a smaller pellet. Number 9s run out of sufficient energy at about twenty-five yards; No. 8½s should be the perfect compromise to nearly forty yards. I would definitely shoot 1⅛ ounce, as I want as many pellets as possible in the pattern.

Chukar Valley

In clay target shooting, this is a commonly thrown presentation. Normally you are placed on a pier overlooking a gully or ravine. You need to shoot this as you normally would a quartering or crossing bird, but with two caveats: go to a larger shot size and increase your choke. You're often shooting at the dome, which is the toughest part of the target. I would say No. 7½s are often more appropriate here than on rabbit targets. If I had chosen improved cylinder for the same bird side-on, I would now change to modified.

Rabbit Targets

Rabbits taken from the edge require No. 7½s, but those taken from the side can be shot with No. 9s to about twenty yards and No. 8s to thirty-five or forty yards. They are most easily broken when airborne, so if that bunny bounces, break it. One key to shooting rabbits is to keep the barrel below the line of the target at your hold point. Never obscure the bird and you shouldn't have much trouble with it. Also, if you shoot a hair low on rabbits on the ground, the pellets will often bounce up and break the target. In other words, be careful not to shoot over the target because the margin of error is greater toward the bottom.

Droppers

These tend to be straightforward, if unusual, targets. After all, it just isn't that often that you're going down with a bird. These stations often have names like "decoying crows." While I have done my share of corvid control, I haven't decoyed them so I just don't know how they come in. Ducks settling into decoys are often shot as droppers, so it does occur in the real world. Still, I doubt that many sporting clay shots have killed enough game as droppers to consider it part of their repertoire.

All you really have to do is apply the same principles we have already discussed, remembering to shoot low and follow through in a downward arc. Often these decoying crow targets are presented so that they suddenly appear above trees in the distance and start to descend. I have heard other shooters recommend shooting straight at them at this point. Sometimes this does work, but I think the habit of shooting with a static gun (i.e., rifling) is a bad habit that should be avoided.

I've also seen single droppers followed by a low, fast quartering or crossing bird on report. In this instance, I try to take the dropper as late as possible so that I can more quickly go to a low hold point to wait for the second target without obscuring it with my barrels. It is a good idea to practice both the decoying crow shot and a flatter incoming target that is descending in the break zone. Sometimes these birds are coming at you and sometimes they're quartering slightly toward you, but it is an easy target to get a feel for if you set it up and practice a little.

Chondels

I have no idea what the derivation of the word "chondel" is. It is probably French for "we were too cheap to buy teal clips." Basically, a chondel is a clay thrown on its side and on a lower arc than a teal target. This low curve should pose no problem. Normally, it is best taken on the rise or close to the top of its arc where it appears to flatten out. Having shot a lot of these birds, I've found that they're often easily broken by intersecting the arc, and keeping a bit below it, near the top—making it a crosser on which you're shooting slightly low. Experimentation and practice will teach you what works best. The good thing about a chondel is that it is a side-on target showing you its entire face. Since you have about fourteen square inches to work with, cylinder will break it a long way off.

Springing Teal

Of all the targets on a sporting clay course, this is the one most likely to get my goat, or to put it another way, to beat me. It really isn't that difficult a target, but I just cannot convince my brain of that. In part, with a high gun mount, my left eye takes over, seeing the target leave the trap and locking onto it; I'm cross shooting. The easiest way for me to compensate is to squint my left eye, but I find this very unnatural.

The best way to deal with this shot is as a trap target going straight up. I shoot them best if I challenge them and take them early, when they're still under power. Leading them feels most natural. Some shooters wait for them to get almost to the top and stall, allowing them to be broken with very little gun movement. The more the target is going away from you, the less lead you will need over or above the bird. If the ascent is quite steep and the target is showing you its top you won't need much choke to break the bird. However, the top is tougher than the bottom of the clay, so if cylinder were right before I would move up to improved cylinder. Also, I would go from No. 9s to 8s when shooting them on the dome.

I think a teal that shows its side is easiest to hit. This is normally presented as a quartering bird if you turn a little bit sideways to it and bring the gun perpendicular to the flight path.

Battues

Battues are very difficult if taken from the side, in most cases because so little surface area is shown. Also, many course designers create a target that is almost out of range until it turns. One of the keys to success is choosing the right hold point. In general, I don't like tracking targets as I feel the shooter is too likely to slow the gun if traveling too far with the bird. The hold point should be just a little bit before the target slows and presents its full face to the shooter. As it starts to slow, mount the gun and shoot as it turns from its edge. For those who shoot maintained lead, which I feel is best for most sporting clay shots, the correct forward allowance is already built in. All you need to do now is drop with the target.

There will be times when you need to shoot the bird a little bit later, perhaps when it is the second target of a simultaneous pair. Now it's dropping like a stone. In that case, make sure you're on the right line and are aggressively moving down. Pull away may prove the most natural for this shot.

Odds and Ends

The sporting clay section is nearly complete; there are just a few more details to consider. First let's return to midis for a moment, where there are three factors that affect success. The first is that midis provide less surface area than a standard target. Second, they travel faster. And third, your brain is attuned to standard clays—and they look just like a slightly smaller standard clay—so you subconsciously think that they're farther away than they really are.

I touched on this earlier, but on sporting clay courses it's a good idea whenever possible to judge the distance of the target by choosing a static object in the break zone and determining how far away it is rather than by judging the airborne target itself. On practice rounds it might be possible, if safe, to actually pace off that distance. Alternatively, you can employ a rangefinder. (I am using one from Bushnell of late.)

Some sporting clay courses are easier than others. And even on relatively difficult courses there are often a couple of easy, or soft, stations. If you get an easy station, revel in it. But don't take it for granted. It is easy to lose focus and concentration and to let a target slip by that just shouldn't. Tournaments, and certainly classes, can be won and lost on easy stations.

Eye Games

Some visual aspects of clay shooting are fair and others are unfair. For example, having a black target flying through dark woods can prove just too difficult for some shooters to see. This just isn't fair. In this circumstance, orange targets should be used.

A quartering target that is curving away from the shooter requires less lead. But if you don't realize what the target is doing, it may take you a long time to work out. This is still fair, albeit difficult. This type of shot should really only be employed in competitions among first-rate shooters. Something similar is a clay target three feet above curved or sloping ground. The shooter initially feels that the target is flat when in fact it is dropping. Competition shooters must learn to recognize this presentation.

Chapter
5

BECOMING A BETTER SHOT

I am quite competitive, but mostly just with myself. If I feel that I'm doing something well, I'm happy. If I feel that I'm not shooting as well as I should be, I'm not a happy camper. Ironically, it is often from these days that I learn the most.

If I miss a single target, I try to let it pass and go on to the next. If, however, I'm having a slump, I try to think why. Indeed, I've been known to talk to myself; not so loudly that neighbors hear, but enough to get curious glances from my loaders.

For me, shooting below par normally revolves around old habits—fiends, not friends. First among them is confidence. Often I know a target is dead right as I start my gun mount. This does not happen often, but when I have this feeling it's close to infallible. If I miss a few birds that I shouldn't and my confidence wavers, I tend to become too deliberate, too exact, looking for the lead. This old habit comes from my clay days—maintained/sustained lead. But when brought over to game shooting this caution translates to a slowing of the barrels, or, perhaps the worse sin of all, double-checking the sight picture by looking at the barrels (or the bead) instead of the bird, which causes the gun to stop.

I recently read somewhere that you must "read the line, feel to lead." This is truly great advice. Yes, there is a sight picture, a gap that varies with speed, distance, angle of the target, and the speed at which you move the barrels. (Accelerating the barrels, or more follow through for maintained-lead shooters, is the key to hitting longer birds.) And this sight picture varies dramatically. Yet shotgun shooting is a hand-eye game, very much like throwing a ball to someone running at full speed. The brain, with training and practice, knows what is correct. With experience, the unconscious mind knows what is best. The kiss of death is to try to make something that works work even better, as that will make you revert to checking your bead, slowing your barrels, and shooting behind the target. When you throw a ball to someone you look at the target, not your hand; it's the same with shooting.

Some of the advice you get from gun scribes and shooting coaches is good, some bad, and some on the borderline of bizarre. Always consider whether the advice offered makes sense for the way you shoot. For example, I recently read a shooting magazine in which a leading coach wrote that he was missing archangels miles in front. He didn't realize it until a picker mentioned it to him after the drive. Actually, I doubt that because birds at sixty yards need loads of lead. More likely he was off-line, but perhaps the advice got him to focus better. Also, I have absolutely no idea how a picker could tell where our expert's shot was going relative to the birds from some distance behind the line.

I recently spent a couple of weeks shooting in Argentina. I could not shoot my way out of a wet paper bag for the first three boxes or so of shells. I was over-leading, but I believe it was for a very curious reason; I am primarily a tall pheasant shot. When you compare the size of the eared dove to even a small hen pheasant, the visual distinctions are dramatic. Subconsciously, I was computing a thirty-yard dove as a sky-high pheasant and dial-

ing in the same lead with which I was accustomed. Also, a pheasant with a tail wind is a much faster target. When I changed my
lead after trial and much error and cut back 60 to 80 percent, my
ratio went from 5 to 1 to 1.2 to 1.

For the remainder of the trip I limited myself to five boxes per
session, as that was as much pounding from my fixed-breech 12-
gauge as I felt comfortable with shooting morning and afternoon,
day after day. A 20- or 28-gauge is sufficient, if properly choked, for
even the tallest dove. I had brought the 12-gauge because on this
trip we were also shooting ducks and geese in different areas. The
heavy loads the outfitter supplied were also unnecessary.

More goofy advice: Another writer suggested shooting low
on classic partridge. Mistakenly thinking that this fellow knew
what he was writing about, I decided to try it on my first day of
partridge shooting last season. I hit my partridge. Low. Too low.
With a fast, low target, just go through the line and shoot, don't
formulate, formalize, or over-think. Partridge are about reactions,
albeit trained, practiced reflexes.

One other bit of odd advice I've heard repeated is to focus
on the air in front of the bird. I beg your pardon? You can only
focus on an object that has reflective qualities, such as the page

Even at a young age, puppies with the right genetic makeup want to point.
Mel and John Pfeifle of Hampshire Kennels and Nancy C. Whitehead Photographer

you're reading or a bird in the air. Don't believe me? Focus out across a field, eyes toward the sky. Try focusing five feet in front, now twenty. No difference, is there? This advice perverts the laws of physics, optics, and cognition. Take it at your own peril. Focus on the bird, see the barrels peripherally, and all will be right with the world.

COACHING AND PRACTICE

Some dog breeds naturally and instinctively point, others retrieve, and still others herd. Man has instincts, as well. Unfortunately, he does not have an instinct to shoot. He must be trained to shoot. It can be coached. It is reactive. Perhaps it is even a conditioned reflex; reward comes in seeing a target break or a bird fold. It is nonetheless a misnomer, almost a malapropism, to call it instinctive. A better way to put it is that the unconscious mind knows better when to slap the trigger than the conscious mind trying to deliberately measure lead. This is true. But this is not instinct.

One shooting coach, who bills himself (a la Sherlock Holmes) as a "shooting consultant," describes the correct lead as about 1¼ inches, ideally measured—get this—off the middle of the sides of the barrel. His logic runs something like this: The gap in real terms increases with the distance from the barrel, the angle formed remaining constant. However, lead as a function of distance is not linear. And this theory doesn't take into account over-unders versus side-by-sides or large versus small gauges, all of which would affect the angle in relation to 1¼ inches because the distance from the side of the barrel in relation to the centerline of the rib keeps changing.

Reading off the middle of the side of the barrel does force you to shoot high, though, which may help on crossers that are often missed low. If you don't pivot your feet there is a physical tendency—running out of swing—to come off-line in a downward arc (rainbowing). But Joe Nickerson's advice, from *The Shooting Man's Creed*, to place a top hat on the bird and shoot for the top is much better. Just keep in mind, for a bird that has set its wings and is dropping ignore this advice and just go through the bird to establish the correct line. A gun that fits is also critical.

An interesting way to practice staying on a true straight line is to try mounting on the line where a wall meets a ceiling, beginning at various times, perhaps 30 to 60 degrees to the front. Try to stay on this line as you mount and move your gun. This is the same line exhibited by a bird in level flight. A right-handed shooter will probably find birds to the left easier if he drops the right shoulder somewhat. Practice keeping your barrels perpendicular to the line. Make this a habit; it is useful.

Practicing your gun mount for five minutes a day will do wonders for your shooting. You'll also discover whether a little bit of weight training might help you. There is no need to go overboard in this regard, but if fatigue takes its toll too early you won't shoot your best.

One of the best bits of advice I've ever received came from legendary shooter Smoker Smith: "Try to make things as easy as possible." With clays, for example, that could mean standing at one side of the cage rather than in the middle or taking the first clay at a spot that makes picking up the second bird of a report pair much smoother. In game shooting, if most birds are coming over your left shoulder you might want to slightly shift your feet and even your gaze to make the shots as easy as possible.

Don't mount the gun too soon because barrel speed often suffers. I've said it before, but it can't be repeated too often: An accelerating barrel kills birds. And an accelerating barrel reduces the required perceived lead in comparison to a maintained lead. If you have two birds coming at you, assuming you're right-handed, take the bird on the right first then go to the bird on the left. This counteracts the tendency of some shooters to take the gun away from the face on the second shot, often more easily done to the right. Always remember to remount, if ever so slightly, when going to a second bird. Just move the gun slightly off your shoulder and face and then bring it back. The stock should hit both areas at about the same time. If the second shot is at the same bird remounting isn't necessary.

I also take issue with the idea that the left hand does most of the work during the mount. If you had to, you could shoot using only your right hand and arm, which keep the gun in the pocket of the shoulder and against the face. (Lift your shoulder so that the gun comes to your face; your face never goes to the gun.) The right hand obviously works the trigger and safety, as well. A left hand that is too active, too dominant, is also likely to move the gun across the face during the shooting process. The left hand is crucial to a good move to the target, but only when working in unison with the right. Many shooters wait with the butt stock too low and the barrels too high for the target; perhaps some instructors emphasize the left hand to counteract this fault.

There are times when the left hand becomes vital for adding follow through. When I was shooting more clays than birds, I toyed with shooting from the hip. Once, when glancing down just on impact I actually saw my left hand speeding the barrels to the right as a form of pull away on a high station at skeet. This was done unconsciously, and after I noticed it, for a while, my consistency vanished. Again, the conscious mind was getting in the way of my reflexes.

We'll take a closer look at the effective range of various chokes in the upcoming chapters, but let me just point out that less choke is better than more choke in most cases. While many shooters mistakenly feel that tight choke kills more cleanly, a bird hit in the back half with a full choke would be cleanly killed with improved cylinder.

Chapter
6

SHOTGUNS AND GUNFIT

Much of the little shooting prowess I possess I owe to the great instructors from whom I've taken lessons. Instruction is a very personal thing and a rapport is of great importance. For this and other reasons I would have to say that I learned much more from some of these gentlemen than others.

It is certainly true that to achieve your potential you will probably need more than one instructor. A friend of mine, Bill Steinkraus, once wrote that in the sport of riding one needs three instructors to reach full potential. All three coaches must be technically correct. The first must instill enthusiasm and love for the sport while not creating bad habits. And he must be someone who gets on well with beginners. The next

This gun displays too much drop and too little cast, forcing the face to be tilted to put the eye over the rib.

instructor takes you to the intermediate or advanced stage. And the third must be a true master to take you to the highest level. This instructor probably never spends any time with beginners.

The instructor who can turn you into a whiz at sporting clays may not be the best choice for something like shooting driven game. Does the instructor communicate in a way that makes things clear for you? When he says something, do you understand it and are you able to implement it?

Sometimes body types play a role. If you're six feet, six inches tall and thin and the instructor is just a hair over five feet tall and stocky, what has worked well for him may not work for you. After we shoot for a while, we all develop habits. If these habits are good and technically correct, we call it style. Many people achieve good success in spite of some bad habits. The question is, If they did things in a more technically correct way would they have achieved more?

I have a friend, Dave, who has amazingly fast reflexes. Dave is quite a good sporting clay shot. But he has two fiendishly bad habits. The first is that he "boxes" his mount. Instead of move-mount-shoot, he mounts, he moves, and then he fires. The other is that instead of turning or pivoting through his waist, he sways. His swaying has a rainbowing effect. And while he does often shoot brilliantly, I am convinced that this habit costs him a couple of birds at most competitions.

In my hubris, I used to think that I could shoot most guns well. The truth is that the better a shot I've become, the more gun-fit matters to me. Last May I traveled to Africa and decided that instead of taking my good guns with me I would borrow one of the camp guns. This autoloader had no cast and was way too short for me; as a result, my shot-to-bird ratio was horrific. Luckily, they had another gun a bit more to my liking, and while I certainly would not have won any prizes with it the disgrace was slightly less.

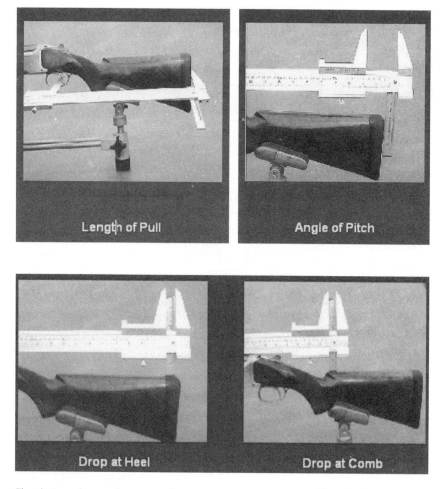

The shotgunning combo gauge allows accurate measurements of length of pull, drop at comb and heel, as well as pitch. Courtesy of Shotgun Combo Gauge

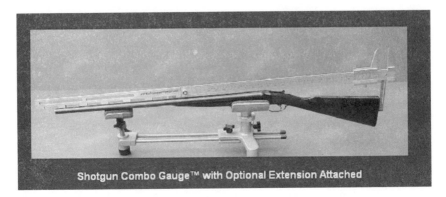

Shotgun Combo Gauge™ with Optional Extension Attached

Photo courtesy of Shotgun Combo Gauge

Which brings us to the point of this discussion: Once your gun mount is consistent, it is imperative to have your gun matched to your physical requirements and style. This doesn't necessarily mean a bespoke (custom) shotgun. Certainly small adjustments can be made by bending or shaving the stock. Pitch and length of pull can easily be adjusted by adding a recoil pad, point of balance can be altered by adding or removing weight to the butt stock, and so on.

Not all gunfitters are created equal. An individual may only be a fair shooting instructor but a first-rate fitter. Similarly, someone could be a great instructor and only a mediocre fitter. When searching for a good gunfitter ask friends and top shots for advice; don't simply go by the reputation of the shooting ground or by the man's ability as an instructor. Merely because someone is associated with a famous gun company or shooting school doesn't necessarily mean that person has sufficient competence. A number of years ago, I sent my better half to one of the really famous shooting grounds near London, with their equally well-known chief instructor. His prescription was sent on to my friends at Beretta, who cut the stock exactly as ordered. Unfortunately, I didn't view it ahead of time. This fellow, either as a typo or a mistake during fitting, had length of pull at 12½ inches. My girlfriend is slight, but she is not a midget. Her correct length of pull is 14 to 14¼ inches. We were forced to sell it on.

There are many nuances of gunfit and gun design that will have a profound effect on your shooting. For example, point of impact. Do both barrels shoot to the same point? Does the gun shoot where you look? Shape of ribs and height are also important. Sometimes, especially on over-unders, changing the rib can make sense. Comb shape and thickness will have a profound influence on nominal cast. Cast is measured from a centerline, but unfortunately this doesn't take into account the thickness of the wood at the comb. Most over-unders are quite thick, but thick combs can be thinned.

Make sure that your fitter makes allowances for your particular gun.

This is also a good time to determine if you like the shape of your grip. If not, a pistol grip often can be turned into a semi-pistol grip. Occasionally, a grip can be straightened out completely. Consider any forend work that needs to be done. For exam-

As the gun is pointed skyward for a high tower shot or driven bird, the thumb comes back towards the nose. The exact opposite occurs if shooting at a target below in a valley where the face tends to move backwards. This is why a driven bird shooter needs a longer length of pull.

ple, a thick forend can be slimmed down or a Schnabel forend tip removed.

If you're having a gun reworked, it would make a lot of sense to shoot it a bit after the alterations have been completed but before it is refinished. That way—trial by fire—you can determine if it needs any additional tweaking.

Too often we accept our limitations or those of our tools. We can all improve through instruction and intelligent practice. But we can also improve our performance and enjoyment by using shotguns whose designs reflect our personal needs and preferences.

ONE GUN FOR EVERY SITUATION?

In *Gough Thomas's Gun Book* the author refers to "appropriate muscular reaction" as the complex muscular reactions that "will move a particular gun of a given weight balance and proportions in a particular way." With this in mind, Thomas became a firm believer in the advantage of sticking to one gun. Others too have echoed this sentiment. It is largely correct.

Recently a friend invited me to his private shooting grounds. He lent me his spare gun, a Gamba Daytona, which had a lovely piece of wood, but the barrels were too heavy and I kept moving it with the same amount of force that I use when shooting my Perazzis. Unfortunately, because of the increased weight of the barrels and my "appropriate muscular reaction," the lead generated by this effort was only half of what I needed. I consistently missed the birds behind. I knew as I fired that my lead was short. Only if I rode the birds, shooting them later than I normally would, could I see the correct lead, develop it, and break the target. I found it quite awkward.

When I moved to the British Isles I would start the season with my Perazzi over-unders on ducks, and as I switched to driven birds I would also switch to a lighter pair of side-by-sides. It

George Digweed is one of the greatest shots of all time, with numerous World Championships and Open titles to his credit. Note the concentration: confidence while simultaneously appearing relaxed. Classic form, winning results.

The tower at Casa de Campo has three levels from which clays are thrown. Mike Rose, formerly the chief instructor at the West London shooting rounds and fitter for Purdey's, ran the facility until he retired recently.

Being able to call well is a good advantage to bringing in ducks. A guide plies his craft near Buenos Aires.

Hypothermia nearly won this day near Shinnecock on Long Island. Charging lions were slightly less dangerous and much more fun!

Salt water offers many opportunities for wildfowlers, but risks are involved. One needs to know what one is doing at all times.

Buck was the best dog that I've ever owned. He handled grouse, woodcock, pheasant, and quail equally well.

This is classic partridge country in Spain at the well-respected Pinos Altos shoot belonging to my friend, Nano Saiz.

My dog, Darky, is getting old like me now, but in his prime he hit the water like the dogs on the ESPN long jump series. Dusty is behind him.

Pepe Fanjul has done much work to improve the quail habitat on his Florida ranch. His guide works the pointers and setters while he works his excellent labs to retrieve the quail. He's one of the safest shots I know.

Yours truly shooting eared dove in Columbia twenty years ago, before the country became too dangerous. The bird boys brought much needed protein back to their local villages.

Extremely classy pointers. If you see dogs this good, and hunt enough to deserve them— and they're for sale—buy them. Mel and John Pfeifle of Hampshire Kennels and Nancy C. Whitehead Photographer.

Dusty passed up a field of dead pheasants to retrieve this runner.

Bob Oliver, Spike Whalen, and I received the trophy for the three-man team flush off the high tower at Casa de Campo from host, Pepe Fanjul.

Clay target games are as much fun for women as they are for men.

Nano Saiz, George Bush, and General Schwarzkopf in Spain.

The grouse butts at Casa de Campo, with sticks to limit swing, create a very realistic and challenging clay presentation.

Tall partridge fly differently than pheasants do, thereby posing different problems for shooters to solve. On this particular Spanish shoot, the birds came so fast that a second loader and a third gun would've been useful.

An extremely tall pheasant curling or slipping on a wind is one of wing shooting's most demanding targets.

Woodcock are highly prized on both sides of the Atlantic. The European species is much larger. Nancy C. Whitehead Photographer.

Woodcock hold particularly well for pointing dogs. This pointer is obviously steady to wing and shot. Mel and John Pfeifle of Hampshire Kennels and Nancy C. Whitehead Photographer.

Duck shooting often occurs in areas of great physical beauty from the Great Lakes to Alaska and from Europe to Africa. This lake is near Buenos Aires, Argentina.

It appears that this shooter is taking a bird just in front of the trees. This wouldn't be a safe shot if beaters were on the hillside. One should always see sky under the bird.

Shotguns come in many configurations and price ranges. Monte Carlo from Franch is a top-of-the line side-by-side.

Beretta's DT 10 is very popular among serious competitors.

Teknys is one of the all time best autoloaders.

would take me a few days of shooting in the beginning years to be as comfortable with one pair as the other, though after a few seasons I found I shot them equally well on any given day. My muscle memory, my brain, whatever you want to call it, learned to subconsciously distinguish between the guns and put the correct amount of effort into each. (The same applies to double triggers; it just works subconsciously.)

Similarly, I'm convinced that if you shoot dramatically different games with different guns the subconscious will adjust to it. For example, if you shoot a lot of trap or skeet and learn to shoot these sports well with guns of the proper configuration you will also shoot your game gun without much adjustment. After all, you're starting these games with the gun premounted.

I recently acquired a very nice Beretta sporting autoloader in 20-gauge. I took it out for its first day of shooting on the skeet range before I made any adjustments to the standard dimensions. It actually comes with spacers that allow drop and cast adjustments to be easily made. Also, I needed more length of pull. Be that as it may, I decided to shoot "gun up" as my mounts were inconsistent. I found my normal hold point to be too far from the trap mouth. Because I normally move-mount-shoot instead of starting with the gun premounted, I found that I developed too much lead too soon and tended to slow down to let the target catch up to me, or rather to my barrels. An interesting anomaly. Once I moved my hold point closer to the house, I started shooting the gun quite well, at least when taking into consideration the less than perfect fit.

As we grow older we all become slightly weaker. To have the same perception of appropriate muscular reaction, the older shooter is often well served to go to a lighter gun. This might mean going from thirty-inch barrels to twenty-seven inches or to a gun with lighter, thinner barrels (albeit with enough wall thick-

Purdey over-unders are among the most desirable guns, both among shooters and collectors. Photo courtesy of Purdey

ness to be safe) or from a 12-gauge to a 20-gauge. Personally, I would choose long, light barrels.

THE OVER-UNDER

My quest for the perfect gun revolves around two issues of equal value. The first is handling. The gun must be alive and move quickly and accurately. Many guns, especially light guns, don't track well. The second consideration is reliability. If the gun doesn't work, most often a flaw of the trigger design, nothing else really matters.

I cannot fathom spending the extraordinary sum necessary for a new pair of London Best over-unders. (If I could afford them, I would go to Purdey.) On the other hand, I cannot handle the sloppy workmanship, especially in final finish, that too often accompanies guns from Spain. My solution would be to buy guns "in the white" there and have them finished by some outstanding craftsman that I know in England.

To describe my perfect over-under, I will start in the front with the barrels and work my way back. In 12-gauge I would have them choked modified and modified, as I tend to shoot tall birds. As these new guns will have single triggers, I see no benefit to different chokes. (Actually, I prefer double triggers, but they are generally not available from the makers I have in mind.) In 20-gauge or 28-gauge, I would choke them improved modified and improved modified. My barrels would be over-bored slightly and the forcing cones lengthened to produce dense, killing patterns. Ideally, they would not be monobloc, where the breech end of both barrels and the lumps are all machined from one solid piece of steel, but rather demibloc, a.k.a. chomper lump, where the barrels are continuous and do not appear sleeved.

The barrels would be between twenty-nine and thirty inches and fairly light. Not so light as to be whippy, but light enough to be quick. I once shot clays in New York State with a friend who owned a number of Holland & Holland sporting trigger lock models. The 12-gauge was a dream to shoot, but the 20s were actually *too* quick, therefore way too whippy. I had to mount in slow motion so I wouldn't blow past and over the targets. Keeping the gun on the right plane, or line, wasn't easy.

I want a gun to handle like a sports car, perhaps a Porsche. The rib would be narrow and solid. Ventilated ribs are supposed to dissipate heat better—not really a consideration for game shooting—but they collect water and dirt. One of the best gunfitters I know sometimes suggests that the shooter put a middle bead on the rib so that he can quickly reference it to see if he's mounting correctly and consistently. It makes no difference for actual shooting, though. Unfortunately, this is unappealing aesthetically and reduces the resale value of the gun. I prefer the smallest, least obtrusive front bead I can find.

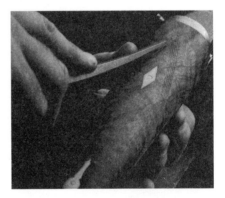

Only master craftsmen are capable of doing the fine work required for Best guns. Nevertheless, one can purchase checkering tools from Brownells and gain great satisfaction working on less important guns. Photo courtesy of Purdey

The trigger guard in my perfect gun would be rolled. (The instructor Mike Rose once told me that he fits Purdey, H&H, and Boss guns with slight differences to length of pull because of trigger guard shape and trigger placement.) The forearm would be slim and the checkering sharp. If the wood were exhibition grade, twenty-six to twenty-eight lines to the inch would be perfect. If less fine wood were used, twenty to twenty-four lines would be about right.

The safety, of course, would be automatic. Always remember that no safety is perfect. You must be vigilant, especially while shooting double guns. When shooting a single gun, always know where your muzzle is pointed on closing.

If the gun were double triggered, obviously I'd want a straight grip. If a single trigger, either a Prince of Wales or a very shallow semi-pistol grip would be best because they give more control. Your grip should be shaped to your individual hand so that the correct part of the finger lines up with the trigger.

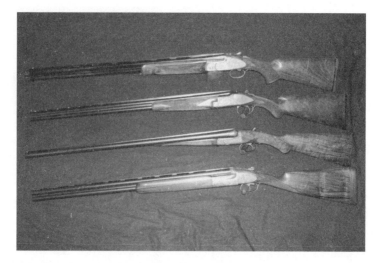

Full pistol grip (top) is most appropriate for target shooting, where complete control is key. Semi-pistol and Prince of Wales grips are preferred for single trigger game guns. The straight grip is best for double trigger guns. Shotguns courtesy of Safari Outfitters

I shoot with quite a bit of cast at the face, and I prefer to keep my head as still and erect as possible. I also prefer a gun that shoots where I look, but I can live with a gun that shoots a hair high, perhaps 55/45 or 60/40 percent above the center of the target. I like my gun to be a little bit shorter than most fitters measure me. Undoubt-

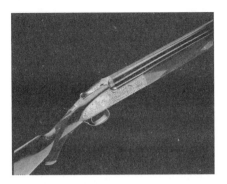

Purdey guns show flawless workmanship. Time to mortgage the house . . . Photo courtesy of Purdey

edly, this is because I am often out in bad weather and am wearing a heavy coat. As long as the cast and drop are correct for the actual length of pull, I find that the length of pull can vary by about half an inch without affecting my shooting. Most fitters measure me between 15⅛ and 15¼, but I typically go with 14⅞ because it seems to work for me in light or bulky clothing.

I would drill a hole and have a trap door cap placed in the middle of the butt so that I could vary the weight with inserts until it balanced exactly the way I wanted. I also would have the gun fitted with a leather-covered recoil pad. If you're sensitive to recoil and shooting heavier loads, you may find a pad with Sorbothane-type material more comfortable.

Let's go back to barrel considerations for a moment. The barrel length needs to fit the shooter. A guy who is six feet, four inches is going to look pretty silly with twenty-five-inch barrels and probably wouldn't shoot them very well, although it would be possible to make the barrels sufficiently heavy (greater wall thickness) if, for example, that balance suited our tall gent. Certainly personal preference is important. My general guideline is that twenty-seven to twenty-eight inches works well for women and shorter men, and thirty inches for bigger or more muscular types.

The length of the barrels makes very little difference in terminal ballistics. Remember, you're shooting a shotgun that throws lots of tiny, more or less round pellets, not a rifle shooting bullets. In the latter case you have a projectile shaped like a missile with a ballistic coefficient where muzzle velocity is affected significantly by the length of the barrel and where muzzle velocity is efficiently translated into retained velocity and energy at significant yardage. But variations in barrel length for shotguns primarily manifest themselves in barrel weight, balance, and handling characteristics, all of which are extremely important.

Barrels, like many old cars, vibrate or flex. This flex tends to be downward. The shorter the barrels, the less the point of impact is affected. This applies more to side-by-sides than over-unders, especially small-gauge side-by-sides—something you need to be aware of when being fitted for small bores.

THE SIDE-BY-SIDE

I'm often asked whether I prefer shooting an over-under or side-by-side. The truth is that I own both and enjoy shooting both. They each have strengths. An over-under tends to weigh more, and therefore can handle the recoil generated by heavier loads. These heavier loads are a decided advantage on extremely tall birds. Because of their weight, over-unders tend to point more consistently than a lighter side-by-side. It is for this reason, rather than the so-called single sighting plane, that I think they do so well in competition. That said, I believe I shoot my side-by-sides better on game than I do my over-unders. The exception being on archangel shoots where 1¼-ounce (36-gram) loads are required.

There is something about a great side-by-side—the way it feels, the way it moves—that few over-unders can match. Part of it is the balance, which tends to be between the hands (where it should be), with the point of balance near the hinge pin. Taking a little wood out at the butt or adding a little lead will get the balance exactly as you prefer. Also, where you like to hold the forend will affect balance.

The fact that a side-by-side tends to weigh three-quarters or perhaps even a pound less than the equivalent over-under also contributes to its liveliness, the naturalness of the way it mounts and goes to the target. The side-by-side is also much quicker to reload than a gun with stacked barrels. This is a function of the size and shape of the gape.

Over-unders are applauded for their single sighting plane. But the truth is that if the gun fits well, the shooter should only be minimally aware of the barrels, seeing them only as a blur. You focus, or should focus, on the target, be it clay or game. Certainly you are aware of the barrels, but you can't focus near and far simultaneously. If you look down the middle of the barrels because that is a natural thing to do (i.e., your mount is correct and the gun fits you), there really is no difference between a narrow or wide sighting plane.

If your gun doesn't fit, and you have to crane your neck to shoot and read the bird off the barrel (I believe the shooter should read the barrel off the bird), perhaps this narrow view produces more "accurate" shooting. I don't dispute the fact that over-unders are better at most clay games. Unfortunately, there is no easy scientific way to establish exactly why. To the best of my knowledge, no top shot uses a side-by-side in competition (the exception being side-by-side competitions, of course). Part of the reason is purely monetary: All shooters can afford an autoloader, most can afford a decent over-under, but very few can afford a Best grade English side-by-side. Also, there are some targets that are undoubtedly easier to read with an over-under.

The Purdey side-by-side will weigh less than the equivalent stack-barreled shotgun and be faster to reload. Photo courtesy of Purdey

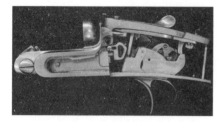

A Purdy's action displays remarkable crafts-manship and complexity. Photo courtesy of Purdey

The intricate forend should not be touched by the average home hobbyist. Photo courtesy of Purdey

The sidelock plate and its internal components. Photo courtesy of Purdey

There are other factors to consider, too. Very few side-by-sides possess reliable single triggers. And side-by-sides recoil differently; over-under shooters tend to get back on target a hair sooner. Neither of these aspects has much effect on the game shot, though.

THE PERFECT SIDE-BY-SIDE

While I like over-unders with long barrels, I prefer twenty-seven to thirty inches for the equivalent side-by-side. The rib should act as an uncon-scious guide to the target, so I prefer it to be concave, which I feel is the subtlest design. Just like on the over-under, I prefer the smallest bead I can find.

Forends come in four designs: beavertail, semi-beaver-tail, splinter, and Spanish splinter, which is almost as

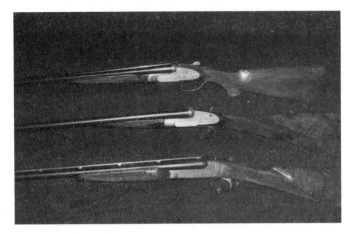

Semi-beavertail, splinter, and beavertail forend types. Personally, I find the semi-beavertail offers the best combination of control and protection from a hot barrel. Shotguns courtesy of Safari Outfitters

wide as the barrels but doesn't come up and around at all. Many American shooters prefer the wide, heavy beavertail, which is very good at protecting your fingers from scalding hot barrels. In this regard, such a forend certainly made sense on old skeet and trap guns, although field guns for game shooting rarely get hot enough for this to matter. Unfortunately, beavertails are ugly things; I find the thickness clumsy because it separates me from the gun and the barrels.

The traditional British shooter prefers the splinter forend, which has a naturally attractive design. Unfortunately, especially on driven shooting or when practicing at clays, the barrels often get hot enough to toast marshmallows. The English have adapted to this by adding a hand guard, normally covered in leather. The hand guard, however, has one serious drawback on driven shoots. When shooting double guns the loader should be, in theory, slapping the gun into your left hand at the hand guard. But hand guards could slip—it happened to me once—which makes this practice dangerous, at least theoretically. If the loader slaps it in farther down toward the action, which safety and logic dictate, it would mean that you would have to readjust your left hand before or during the mount.

On one occasion when shooting a single gun with a hand guard I found myself taking off the left wing of driven pheasant that were overhead and relatively low. After this happened three or four times in a row, I realized that the top opening in the hand guard surrounding the rib was slightly off-center. Subconsciously I was reading off this gap, and it was affecting my point of impact. After I removed the hand guard I went on to have one of my best shooting days ever, at least in terms of cartridges to birds.

My favorite forend is the Italian semi-beavertail. It is aesthetically pleasing, exceedingly practical, and it offers a good deal of protection, especially when combined with a shooting glove. At the same time, it connects the hand to the barrels—just where it should be. About twenty years ago I bought a Piotti King that had a slim semi-beavertail and since then I have had it copied for all of my side-by-sides.

One of the reasons that side-by-sides move so well is that their barrels tend to be light. If you're purchasing a used side-by-side, always check the wall thickness of the barrels with a gauge designed specifically for this task. Sufficient thickness is the key to not losing fingers, or worse. Worn-out barrels are most commonly found in English guns. My friend Tony Seth Smith, one of the truly great professional hunters of Africa, has a lovely pair of old Hollands. Unfortunately, when shooting one day a good deal of the barrels went flying past his face. He was lucky to escape injury, but the gun required re-barreling.

Arguably the best and most famous American outdoor writer over the last half of the twentieth century was a fellow named Jack O'Connor. He was a childhood hero who knew a tremendous amount about big game hunting, rifle shooting, and rifles, but I've always had my doubts about his authority on the subject of shotguns. In his classic book, *The Complete Book of Rifles and Shotguns,* he stated the following: "The best doubles are made with selective single triggers that give the shooter the option of firing either barrel first. They also have automatic ejectors that throw out fired shells . . . the cheaper doubles have two triggers—one for each barrel—or nonselective triggers that always fire the open or un-choked barrel first."

O'Connor was the dean of American gun writers in the 1950s and '60s, but I cannot help but think that his exposure to English Best guns must have been limited. The fact is that few gun makers made decent single triggers in those days, and even fewer do now. Double triggers are almost infinitely more reliable on side-by-sides. Single triggers do work on American guns such as the Winchester Model 21, but they rarely work well when coupled with the complex actions of a sidelock. Still, no one would call a Purdey or Boss side-by-side with double triggers a "cheap" gun; the base price for one of these guns is probably in the neighborhood of a hundred thousand dollars.

This is a long way to go to get to some simple advice: Buy double triggers. They work. They also give you an instant selection for which barrel to fire first. I think it is actually exceedingly rare for anyone to change the selector on his barrel for a particular bird because it's typically awkward and slow. This greatly reduces the usefulness of a selector. Selectors can be changed ahead of time, of course, if you're doing something like shooting at ducks coming in over decoys or shooting driven grouse on gun number one, where you want the tighter barrel to fire first.

The trigger guard should be rolled, and the front trigger hinged. A straight grip works most naturally with a double trigger, although some shooters prefer a very shallow semi-pistol or Prince of Wales grip. A Prince of Wales grip adds a degree of extra control on small-bore guns, namely the 28-gauge and .410.

Beretta, Perazzi, and Krieghoff all offer triggers that can be moved forward or back. This allows for the trigger to be aligned with the correct part of the finger. Photo courtesy of Beretta

Side-by-sides are, to my way of thinking, more natural for shooting game in small gauges than over-unders. For one thing, the greater mass of a side-by-side's barrels is very helpful in picking up a bird, especially in a wooded background. (Remember, I never suggested that you don't see your barrels; I just meant that you don't focus on them or be consciously aware of their presence.)

Length of pull is a critical dimension in shotgun fitting, and there are two elements to consider: the distance from your hand to the middle of the butt and the distance of your index finger from your grip to the trigger. Say, for example, that your correct length of pull is fifteen inches. If your gun has a very tight pistol grip it is conceivable that while the overall length coincides with the formula of your fitter, the distance between the trigger and the forced placement of your hand does not allow the last digit of the index finger to be placed properly on the trigger. (Perazzi and a few other manufacturers have dealt with that consideration by manufacturing a trigger that can be moved forward and backward, a very nifty idea.) This is actually a more common problem for stack barrels or other guns with a full pistol grip, as side-by-sides typically have a straight grip.

This ingenious system of Beretta's allows the use of spacers to change drop and cast.
Photo courtesy of Beretta

Side-by-side enthusiasts must deal with two other problems. First is "down flip," the tendency of thin whippy barrels to flip downward on firing. This is exacerbated by longer barrels and smaller gauges. In general this is remedied by having less drop at comb. The second problem, if your original fitting was for an over-under, is that the wood at the comb is thinner and therefore needs modification to the gunfit to get the cast right.

THE AUTOLOADER

Autoloaders have many reputations, some of which are justified and some of which are unfounded. For instance, they have a reputation for jamming, for being intrinsically less safe, and for being unrefined, clumsy tools compared to an elegant side-by-side. The plain truth is that they can shoot very well and are more pleasant to shoot in terms of recoil than the equivalent double guns. The latter is true because the gas mechanism on an autoloader actually reduces recoil or spreads it over time, so that instead of getting punched hard in the shoulder you are only gently

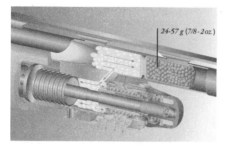

24-57 g (7/8 - 2 oz.)

The modern gas mechanism can handle a wide array of shot charges. The gas mechanism creates more of a shove than the slap of a fixed breech gun. Photo courtesy of Beretta

pushed. For anyone who shoots hundreds of rounds in a day at competition, this is a great advantage.

If you hunt wildfowl in salt or brackish water or shoot steel or Hevi-Shot loads an autoloader cannot be beat. Companies such as Beretta and Benelli even have models available with camo synthetic stocks. Recently I have been playing with a Beretta Teknys 20-gauge sporting with competition chokes and a stock adjustable for drop and cast; it is the best autoloader I've ever shot, and even the wood is pretty.

My first shotgun at age twelve was a Browning Auto 5 in 12-gauge. Luckily, I was a big kid and the recoil was never a problem. This gun was probably one of the best of its kind for its day, but that day has long since passed. The barrel slid back, forcing open the action, its movements regulated by a long spring and a couple of rings that, depending on how they were placed, determined whether the gun was set to handle heavy or light loads. Its real disadvantage in modern terms was that the high hump on the stock created a lot of drop at comb. Thinking back, I'm not sure how I shot it.

My next gun was a Remington 1100 that I bought in the first few years of manufacture. This gun was eminently

Some start young: The author about forty years ago.

more shootable, and my scores at skeet improved dramatically. Also, being gas operated, it was much more comfortable to shoot.

To my mind, the two biggest problems with an autoloader are poor finish and poor stock design. I suppose a third issue would be sloppy triggers, although this is less universal than the other two faults. When I say poor stock design, what I really mean is that the gun makers try to make one size stock fit all shooters. Recoil pads allow you to easily alter length of pull and pitch, but drop at comb and cast at face had, for the longest time, been ignored. (Beretta has recently added spacers that allow drop and cast to be altered to an individual's requirements.) The more I shoot, the more I'm convinced that adjusting yourself to an ill-fitting stock causes a host of problems.

In an effort to save money (not totally unjustifiable considering how hard it is for a gun company to make a profit), gun makers frequently went to cheap wood with "pressed" checkering and a hard polyurethane finish. This gave what would otherwise have been quality guns a less than pleasing look. To their credit, many gun makers today have returned to cut checkering, or at least something that looks like cut checkering, and wood with a bit more grain. I have nothing against guns with fiberglass or Kevlar stocks, by the way. When matched with barrels of the same camo pattern, they are great in a duck or goose blind.

Drop at comb and cast can be altered by shaving away wood. Combs on autoloaders are so thick that shaving is straightforward. If

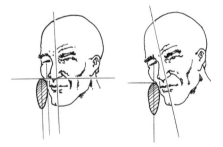

One size doesn't fit all. Many American shotguns were made with zero or minimal cast, forcing the shooter to cock his head and place his master eye over the center line.

you do this it makes sense to refinish the stock at the same time and, if you're so inclined, to re-cut the checkering. If the comb is too low moleskin or other padding can be added to lift it. Indeed, that is what I did with my old Remington 1100. The pad I used was manufactured by Meadowlands Industries and had glued Velcro attachments for the side of the butt stock. Small inserts of various heights could be placed on the comb and under the pad. By moving these inserts slightly to the side, I very inexpensively altered my cast.

Many autoloading shotguns come with marginal triggers. I don't consider the trigger that has a heavy pull to be a problem because if it is free of creep and slack it can easily be lightened. A number of companies that cater to clay target shooters will rework triggers to be light and crisp and good enough for competition. A trigger pull of about three pounds is ideal on a target gun; three and a half to four is acceptable. And three and a half to four and a half for a field gun is about correct, with the second trigger weighing roughly another pound. If for some reason your trigger can't be reworked, it can always be replaced. Aftermarket triggers have been available for decades.

One of the keys to keeping an autoloader in good working order is to know how to clean it well. Read the owner's manual and if you have any questions consult a local gunsmith about your particular firearm. My old Remington 1100 has a couple of gas ports along the barrel. I found that cleaning them occasionally with a pipe cleaner kept the gun working forever. Also, plastic can build up in the chamber and slow or stop ejection. Just use a chamber brush to deal

Recoil reduction systems change the balance and dynamics of the shotgun. While added weight will reduce recoil, you may want to add a weighted forend cap to preserve balance and handling. Photo courtesy of Beretta

with this. Some guns work best if kept slightly "wet" with a spray of gun oil along the spring area of the outside surface of the magazine tube.

I haven't belonged to the Skeet Association for two decades, but when I did, if memory serves, 12-gauge autoloaders dominated that event. In the sub-gauges it was tube-set guns, especially light K-80s, that did most of the winning. This reveals that recoil was a considerable concern even to the top shooters. If you have to shoot 250 straight just to get into the shoot-off, as is common in major American competitions, and do that week in and week out, recoil and flinching, its evil twin, are going to be a concern.

So if you shoot a lot at clays and are doing so in the 12-gauge events, an autoloader should be in your battery of firearms. Even if you own expensive firearms, it makes sense to have an autoloader for days when it's wise to leave fine guns at home. Shooting ducks in saltwater marshes would be a prime example.

Chapter

7

THE TRUTH ABOUT CHOKES AND PATTERNING

There is a common misconception that shotgun patterns spread in an even, cone-like fashion. This tends only to be true for improved cylinder choke.

Cylinder opens up very quickly, as does skeet. Full tends to stay very tight for quite a distance and then spreads dramatically. Strangely, at very close range full produces a wider pattern than modified. If you go to a patterning board and shoot modified and full at five yards you will find that the full choke produces the bigger pattern. This is almost like a trick done with mirrors. At five yards there are deformed pellets on the fringe of the pattern caused by the effect of increased choking. These flyers are of no consequence and, in fact, dissipate very rapidly; in the next five yards or so they are gone.

At roughly fifteen or twenty yards cylinder choke is producing a pattern of roughly thirty inches. Full at twenty yards, give or take an inch or so, produces a pattern that is barely ten inches wide. Roughly 700 square inches versus 78 inches, or nearly nine times the margin of error, is gained by lessening the choke at this distance. Certainly there are times and situations where a twenty-yard shot is sporting, but a bird hit with a tight choke at that range won't be fit table fare, whereas one shot with an open choke usually is.

Much of what I know about patterns comes from shooting sporting clays, where breaking just a few more targets can make the difference between a win and a loss. Clays, like gamebirds, provide shots where great energy or penetration is required. As mentioned earlier, a clay is toughest on its dome and most fragile on its underbelly. So a clay quartering away and rising slightly, or a target shot from above, needs more choke and larger pellets than a clay thrown from a high tower that is exposing its most vulnerable surface. Likewise, a pheasant that flushes and flies away from the gun requires much more penetration to reach a vital organ than the same bird driven over the gun (which exposes its head, spinal column, and vital organs).

Cylinder is hard to beat for the first shot on walked-up grouse or woodcock, or even quail when they hold well. If your target is typically twenty-five to thirty-five yards away improved cylinder is far and away the best, most efficient selection. Modified works well and will extend the range at which you could humanely bring down the bird, but it provides less margin of error.

Sir Joe Nickerson was certainly lethal with his 28-gauge guns in his later years, but he did admit to using more choke than he recommended to others. Able to center his targets, he did not need the greater margin of error available with less choke or a larger gauge. (The size/diameter of the dense pattern diminishes as gauge gets smaller.) I know one shooter who is absolutely lethal with his little 28-gauge Perazzi, but he has it choked extra full and extra full; very dense, but also very little margin of error.

A pheasant taken over a pointing dog is generally shot at fairly close range, assuming you have a good steady dog. Improved cylinder choke is probably ideal for this type of shooting, giving a fairly good margin of error and not damaging too much meat. While some shots will be crossers and some quartering, many will be going away. Since I want a load that will kill humanely in the most difficult situation, I would probably opt for No. 4 or 5 shot.

Now let's look at the same scenario using a springer spaniel, which is more likely to flush the bird for a longer shot. Here I would want improved cylinder and modified or improved cylinder and full. If I were using one of my own Labs, brilliant dogs for picking up, but only marginally trained for flushing work, I would probably choose modified for my first barrel.

Next, let's look at driven partridge. This is a small bird compared to a pheasant so you need more shot in the pattern to ensure hits in a vital area. As always, choke and load must be taken together. Number 7s (No. 7½s U.S.) and cylinder to improved cylinder choke are perfect for traditional partridge shooting. For tall partridge—the sky-high perdiz available on the best drives at places like La Flamenca, La Cuesta, Ventosilla, or Casa Sola—No. 6s are necessary to have enough downrange energy and modified choke or more is needed to create dense patterns.

Medium to large ducks obviously take a lot of killing. Your pellets must penetrate dense plumage, a layer of fat, and thick muscle. With a lead or Hevi-Shot paradigm, No. 5 or 6 shot is my favorite for decoyed birds, and No. 3 or 4 for pass shooting. I use very little choke for decoyed birds, more for pass shooting. These days I highly recommend Hevi-Shot as a lead substitute because it kills like nobody's business. There is a caveat, though. I have been told that the nominal choke should be a modified or less, as you will shoot dense patterns in this configuration. I do not suggest using Hevi-Shot in fine, old guns. (I suppose that's why Mr. Browning invented autoloaders, which also help tame the recoil they generate.)

Too much choke: The inner circle represents full choke and the outer improved cylinder, which means a bird shot at too close a range with too much choke (full) will be mortally wounded but not killed cleanly. The wider distribution of pellets (improved cylinder) is a great advantage to nearly forty yards.

PATTERNING FOR CLAYS

A thirty-inch patterning circle has two interior circles, one at about 17½ inches and the next at about 24½ inches. Each of these three circles is of equal area. Ideally, there would be a hundred pellets in each of the circles, which would make it theoretically impossible for a clay or gamebird to fly through unscathed. (Clays are often hit without showing a "visible piece" because sufficient energy was not imparted. This is where shot size and distance considerations take over.) In a perfect world, I would further divide the circle into quarters to produce twelve geometric zones of equal area, and there would be twenty-five pellets in each zone. Dream on.

The following chart shows the way pellets spread at different yardage with different chokes. Spread is related to sufficient density to break a side-on clay. These numbers are approximate but useful; all barrel/load combinations are unique. A clay from the bottom (or pheasant for that matter) requires less density and choke.

Distance	Cylinder	Improved Cylinder	Modified
10 yards	21"	12"	–
15 yards	27"	17"	–
20 yards	30"	21"	17"
25 yards	30"	25"	24"
30 yards	20"	30"	25"
35 yards	9"	19"	27"
40 yards	–	16"	27"
45 yards	–	–	27"

*These spreads and densities were taken from the video *Optimum Performance, Chokes and Loads.*

THE WORLD OF BARRELS, TUBE SETS, AND CHOKE ACCORDING TO BRILEY

In the 1970s a fellow named Claude Purbaugh started making the first sub-gauge tube sets for the skeet shooting community. In a matter of minutes a 12-gauge gun could be converted to 20 or 28 or .410. In 1975, Noel Winters used a set in his Krieghoff to become the world skeet champion—shooting the same gun in all four events. (I understand that he did not use carrier barrels to keep the weight and balance close, as is often the case today.)

The tubes were an all-aluminum product and did not feature integral ejectors. The shooter had to literally remove the 12-gauge ejector from the gun and insert an extra set of ejectors in the appropriate gauge that were modified to match that specific set of tubes. This was especially cumbersome with spring-loaded ejector guns such as those from Beretta and Perazzi.

135

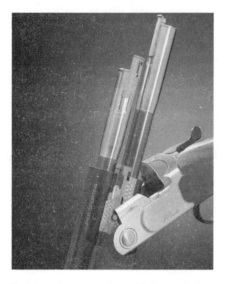

Stan Baker was one of the early pioneers in making interchangeable choke tubes. Jess Briley was another. Briley helped create the revolution and fostered the evolution in tube sets. His tubes were made from two materials: stainless steel for the chambers and aluminum for the barrels. The stainless chambers allowed the use of integral ejectors, which made it possible to quickly and easily change gauges. These tube sets also have interchangeable chokes.

Modern sub gauge tubes with integral ejectors allow one to quickly change sets. Photo courtesy of Briley

The early sets were quite heavy; the .410 tubes weighed 1½ pounds. The newer Briley ultra-lites only weigh ten ounces per set. This was accomplished by replacing the stainless chambers with titanium and by intelligently creating high-tech barrel profiles, which reduce the mass of the barrel as the pressure decreases.

Briley is a serious company now, with many employees and state of the art equipment. It started, however, in the back of a garage with Jess working on a mill and Cliff Moller working on a honing machine. For his first three years at Briley, Cliff's job was to hone in jug chokes. "It was an expensive way to do the work, and it was also fairly unpredictable going from one barrel to another. Sometimes the results were quite good and other times not at all, so the lengths of the diameter would have to be played with to get the barrels to pattern well. It was just an inherently inconsistent way to work."

Chokes are actually pretty complicated, and the length of the screw-in choke affects performance.

In their early days Briley reviewed the barrels of a lot of manufacturers and found a great variation between them. "Some were three inches and parallel, and some were only two inches in parallel length," noted Cliff. "It was as though the manufacturers were buying one length of sleeve and cutting it back. While you can do almost anything with screw-in chokes you couldn't do a lot with the conical end of fixed chokes.

"On a custom basis it is very difficult to modify the conical section of a fixed choke because tapered reamers have a tendency to chatter and cut eccentrically. However, some manufacturers, for example, Browning, did produce a long conical section in their fixed choked barrels (probably roller forged). Most manufacturers traditionally used relatively short conical sections in their fixed choked barrels."

Bore-to-diameter ratios are critical when determining the manufacturing cost of a choke. The shorter versions are less expensive to manufacture. "When you use a boring bar you need to control the chatter of the tool," says Cliff. "The farther you extend the cutting tool, the more it wants to vibrate. One uses the thickest bar possible to cut down on vibration."

In 12-gauge shotguns, chokes start to become expensive to manufacture when they are longer than 2.2 inches (3-to-1 bore-to-diameter ratio). As length of choke increases, the manufacturing difficulty increases exponentially. As Moller points out, "During the development stage we

Modern choke tubes are very different from earlier versions and new materials are also available. Photo courtesy of Briley

spent a lot of time determining what was the nominal length to make our chokes achieve the best performance. How long should it be? How long should the conical section be? How long should the restrictive section be? How much gap clearance should we allow? (The gap clearance is the difference in diameter between the bore of the shotgun and the seat of the choke where they mate up.)

"Another highly critical detail is insuring that the choke counter bore (the machined geometry where you screw in the choke) is absolutely lined up perfectly within .0015 Total Indicator Run-out. (That is fancy language that means the counter bore needs to be machined in line and concentric with the bore of the shotgun barrel.)

"We discovered that a choke length of 2¾ inches was ideal. It features 2 inches of transition length (conical section) and ¾ inch of restrictive diameter length (choke). If the gap clearances are kept at a minimum it produces the best and most consistent results. Another reason for designing a long choke is to compensate for any small error that might occur in the installation over a longer surface area, neutralizing most of the negative effects of error by minimizing them. Longer choke produces a longer transitional area before the restrictive diameter. It gives more room to compensate for the small error that might occur in the installation of screw chokes. That error should be no more than one and a half thousandths — a very close tolerance.

"Weird things can occur with silly conical or restrictive lengths. Restrictive lengths that are too long generate poor open patterns. Super-short restrictive lengths generate extremely inconsistent patterns. For example, if 2¾ is good, isn't 3½ better? No. It doesn't hurt but it will not perform better 99.99 percent of the time. We do make chokes longer than 2¾ for other utilitarian purposes, such as color-coded extended chokes. This makes things easier for fast changes of a great selection of chokes.

"Over-boring or back-boring: We have found that over-bored barrels produce excellent patterns for cylinder to light full chokes. One has to work a little harder to get super-tight patterns from over-bored barrels. It is possible, just more difficult. On the other hand, under-bored barrels with small-bore diameters (.718–.723) resist producing good open patterns in cylinder or skeet but do generate tight patterns rather easily.

"There are other advantages to over-boring, including less recoil. Public enemy number one of a competition shooter is recoil. If you want to end your career fast, develop a flinch. So if you are fighting recoil and want tight patterns use an over-bored gun and screw in your tightest Briley chokes. I doubt you will outperform the efficiency of our chokes. In games like sporting clays, skeet, and trap, over-bored guns are ideal for the vast majority (range) of targets."

When asked about forcing cones, that area of the barrel between the chamber and the bore (I.D., or internal dimensions/diameter) that tapers to "seal" gases behind the wad and shot, Cliff said, "The standard forcing cone is 5 degrees. We believe that the ideal is between 2 and 2½ degrees."

They aren't big fans of longer cones for two reasons:

"First is safety. The barrel profile of O.D. (outer dimensions) begins to thin out and if you extend the forcing cones you start to compromise the safety of the barrel. Second is that we have yet to see any benefit of forcing cones longer than 2 degrees."

For shooting the most modern loads of tungsten or steel Moller recommends light modified or modified chokes.

Chapter

8

PSYCHEDELIC SHOTGUNNING

I love LSD. No, I'm not a drug addict. What I'm referring to is Load Specific Density. Never heard the term? Guess what, I just coined it. This isn't the number of pellets in the thirty-inch circle as a function of the number of pellets in the load, but rather as the total minimum number necessary to kill efficiently. The more modest the load, the greater the density required to kill humanely.

Most shooters define a 40-percent pattern at thirty yards as cylinder choke, 50 as improved cylinder, 60 as modified, and a 70 or more as full. This really doesn't matter much to me, as it reveals very little. Obviously, I'm better off in terms of the number of pellets on target with 40 percent of the 1¼-ounce load than I am with 50 percent of a one-ounce load. I will just have more pellets on target, which is really what I'm after when I'm trying to bring down game. Fifty percent is defined as improved cylinder regardless of whether you're shooting a small or large load, yet obviously there are many more pellets in the latter load.

Now I'm really going to confuse the issue. What choke is really telling me, or at least what I care about, is my overall spread, which translates into margin of error. For example, a full

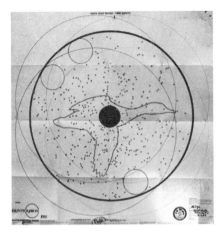

Only by patterning a gun will you see what it really does with different loads. Do remember this is a two-dimensional depiction of a three-dimensional event. Even with some gaps, as long as they're not clustered in one area in a consistent manner, a bird flying through the pattern may be cleanly killed. This is a skeet load courtesy of Remington and patterned at the appropriate yardage.

choke at twenty yards in a 12-gauge shotgun produces approximately a ten-inch-diameter circle for the pattern. The improved cylinder choke produces a twenty-inch circle. And at the same distance cylinder and skeet push thirty inches. Since the area of the circle is πr^2 squared, I actually have four times the margin of error when shooting improved cylinder over full choke at that distance. This is what I want. This is just dandy. As gauge is reduced, useful diameter/spread of pattern shrinks somewhat. (By the way, none of this is relevant to the .410.)

But for the range at which I shoot my birds, I want the maximum density of pellets on target, with the sole caveat being that I don't want so many pellets that I overly destroy meat. As I'm talking about shooting birds at over thirty-five yards, the destruction of tissue is minimal.

So when I say that I want improved cylinder, or quarter choke in British nomenclature, to almost forty yards, my real implication is that I desire the *spread* of this choke to that distance. If, however, my improved cylinder choke actually patterns at 50, 60, or 70 percent, so much the better because my "lethality factor"—the number of pellets × the energy of each pellet—is also increased. I want margin of error that equals spread, but with

greater density than nor-
mally associated with nominal choke nomenclature.

There are two ways to
improve performance. One
is simple: better shotshell design; the other is more difficult: barrel modification. A
pellet, to be aerodynamic,

The wad and petals separating from the shot. Courtesy of Remington

needs to be round or spherical and needs to stay round as it travels down the barrel and on to the target. (Pellets mass produced
for shotgun cartridges are never truly round, but you need pellets that are somewhat close.) The amount of antimony, which
determines the hardness of the pellet, is the single most important factor in keeping them round en route. When the primer
ignites and the pellets start to push down the barrel there is a
tendency for those pellets closest to the rear to compress. In so
doing, they lose their roundness and are much more likely to fly
away from the main mass of the pattern. Similarly, pellets on
the side have forces exerted on them by the forcing cones. The
sharper the angle of the forcing cones, the greater the deformation. Higher antimony content reduces this tendency, as do
plastic shot collars. This "squish factor" comes into play again
just before the pellets depart the barrels due to the effect of
choke. There is also barrel scrub deformation, and sometimes
not all pellets are protected by the petals of the wad, especially
in small bores.

Plating is an advantage if, and only if, the antimony level is
high, and it is truly electroplated. Most companies merely "wash"
their plating over the lead.

As all the pellets are pushed together by the forces from behind and to the sides, pellets are deformed. These less spherical

The modern shotshell. Courtesy of Federal Cartridge

pellets not only string out, but because they're less aerodynamic they provide less energy on target, if they get that far.

In addition to starting off with a hard, round pellet, you can dramatically reduce the tendency of pellets to compress through the use of a buffering agent. I believe Winchester was the first company to offer commercially buffered loads with an agent they called Grex. Tom Roster, the reloading guru, achieved amazingly dense patterns by using baking flour as the buffering agent for a 1¼-ounce load.

With the exception of shooting very tall birds, you don't really need such a heavy payload. You can maximize a standard one-ounce load to kill at fairly great range—forty-five yards or so—if one can get patterns of over 80 percent.

The other way to create denser loads is by altering barrel specifications. This is where it gets tricky. Sporting clay guys have been working a long time with lengthening forcing cones, over-boring barrels, and other tricks of the trade designed to create the most even, densest patterns by reducing factors from the sides that deform pellets.

Forcing cones were designed in the days of paper/felt wads. Their job was to seal the gas on one side of the wad from the pellets on the other. To this end, they narrowed rapidly over a distance of about ⅜ inch.

The advent of the modern plastic shot cup has changed the dynamics of interior ballistics. For one thing, the sides of the plastic wad's shot collar expand outward, enabling wider bore dimensions to be employed while maintaining the seal. The wider the bore, the less the pressure exerted on the pellets. The longer the forcing cones, the less pressure on the pellets; the fewer number of deformed pellets, the greater the number reaching the target in a round (sort of) shape. The best of both worlds are achieved. The spread of, say, improved cylinder with the density of improved modified choke can be achieved.

Now here's the bad news: You have to be very careful about altering barrel dimensions. While many over-unders and autoloaders possess barrel thicknesses that allow over-boring, fine English guns certainly do not—at least not if you want to keep them in proof. Lengthening forcing cones is another matter. Many guns do have enough metal and wall thickness in this area to allow a gentler angle. Depending on who you read and who you believe, and depending probably even more on the particular barrel and the particular gunsmith, patterns 10 to 30 percent denser can be achieved. In regard to proof, it is my understanding that lengthening forcing cones won't take a gun out of proof the way, say, lengthening chambers will. Don't take this as gospel, though. Always consult the manufacturer, the relevant proof house, and a competent gunsmith *before* having any work done.

Many sporting clay companies are providing guns specifically for that market with long forcing cones and over-bored barrels. Adding hard, round, buffered loads could easily create a combination that would make many 28-gauge guns outperform some 12s.

As I go down in size, I increase the nominal amount of choking. For example, if I feel modified choke is right in 12-gauge, I would switch to improved modified in 20-gauge and full in 28-gauge. Also, to achieve sufficient density, I would probably switch from my favorite No. 5 to No. 6 shot as pellet numbers decrease.

The following chart shows how much more dense, or efficient, a lighter load must be to keep up with the paradigm of 1¼ ounces at various chokes.

Shot/Load (#5 U.K., #6 U.S.)	Total Pellets	Density	Pellets in Circle
Cylinder Choke			
#5, 1¼ oz.	280	45%	126
#5, 1⅛ oz.	250	50%	125
#5, 1 oz.	225	55%	125
#5, ⅞ oz.	200	63%	125
#5, ¾ oz.	170	74%	125
Skeet Choke			
#5, 1¼ oz.	280	50%	140
#5, 1⅛ oz.	250	56%	140
#5, 1 oz.	225	62%	140
#5, ⅞ oz.	200	70%	140
#5, ¾ oz.	170	82%	140
Improved Modified			
#5, 1¼ oz.	280	65%	180
#5, 1⅛ oz.	250	72%	180
#5, 1 oz.	225	80%	180
#5, ⅞ oz.	200	90%	180
#5, ¾ oz.	170	–	–
Full Choke			
#5, 1¼ oz.	280	70%	196
#5, 1⅛ oz.	250	78%	196
#5, 1 oz.	225	87%	196

*All numbers are approximate in regard to the number of pellets in the load because actual pellet diameter varies from company to company, and sometimes from lot to lot within the same company.

As you can see, it is the last number that reveals the most. The percentage tells me how much density, as choke, that I need to achieve my number. The lighter loads must be extremely efficient to achieve a similar number of pellets in the circle as the 1¼-ounce load. I have had many factory choked guns that produced patterns of over 80 percent, but none that beat 87 percent. The rest is up to you, a flock of different cartridges, and a patterning board.

A thirty-inch circle includes about seven hundred square inches. For me, the optimum would be 80 percent with a 1¼-ounce load—225 pellets, with one pellet per three square inches.

PENETRATION VERSUS DENSITY

Much has been written about the relative importance of penetration and density. To my mind, they are equally important and should be viewed together. However, if one has an edge over the other it would be penetration, which is obviously a function of energy. After all, it does no good to hit the bird with a hundred pellets if the pellets themselves can't reach the organs to do vital damage.

John Bond, writing in the British magazine *The Shooting Gazette*, states the following:

"To be reasonably sure of killing a pheasant, the bird must be hit by four pellets, each of which carries an energy of 0.86 foot-pounds. To achieve this, the pattern in the 30-inch circle at the range you hit the bird must contain at least 30 pellets. This has been worked out from the area covered by the bulk of the pheasant's body compared to the area covered by a 30-inch circle. The energy has been worked out from the simple penetration tests that show that less energy than this can produce superficial damage. The bird may still be pricked but it is unlikely to be killed.

"No. 5 (No. 6 U.S.) shot carries this energy to about 62 yards; No. 6 shot carries this energy to 55 yards; No. 7 shot carries this energy to about 45 yards."

Now I'm not sure I agree with any of this. First, 0.86 seems awfully low to me. It is what No. 9 pellets display at about twenty-five yards—also the point at which No. 9s can no longer be counted on to break clays consistently. For example, No. 7½ target loads show this much energy, according to the standard performance charts, at about sixty yards. Yet no one would suggest 7½s for sixty-yard birds.

There is another caveat as well: Shotgun pellet performance charts are intrinsically inaccurate. This is due to a number of factors, including the variation in size and roundness. There is a lot of leeway in the industry standards for pellets that are marked as a certain size. Also, even in the same batch, or even in factory loaded shells, there will often be some variation among the pellets of a single cartridge. So it is reasonable to presume that your load is less efficient than the charts depict unless your pellets are bigger; i.e., at the upper limit of the industry standard for that size pellet.

I'm also not so sure about the "thirty pellets" rule. I did read somewhere—for the life of me I can't remember where—that thirty pellets, perfectly evenly distributed, would be the theoretical minimum to ensure clean kills in a pattern. But I have never seen this distribution in the real world. To consistently kill a pheasant-sized bird, something closer to one hundred pellets is probably necessary within the circle. Preferably more.

A 1¼-ounce load contains roughly 280 No. 6 pellets. Eighty percent of the pellets would be 224, and if you can achieve this number in the circle at forty yards you stand a good chance of having a hundred pellets left at something between fifty and sixty-five yards, depending on your gun and load.

My own experience, and I have killed tens of thousands of pheasants, is that thirty-five yards is the maximum range for No. 6s U.K. (approximately No. 7s U.S.). They just don't have enough energy past that distance, and may even be marginal at that range.

To kill humanely for extreme shooting you must know the capabilities of your gun and your cartridge. But more important even than the capabilities of your gun are your own capabilities. While most shooters who are willing to practice on high towers under the scrutiny of a first-rate coach can become reasonably competent shots at forty yards, it is only the rare individual who by virtue of talent or dedicated practice can reliably kill farther out than this.

Being a true sportsman means keeping crippling to a minimum. It therefore behooves all of us to honestly appraise our own shooting and determine what is and what is not a sporting shot.

Chapter
9

THE LAST WORD ON
NONTOXIC SHOT

It has been a very long time since anyone in the shooting world has been able to impress me with their store of knowledge the way Tom Roster did. I first learned about Tom when I read Bob Brister's excellent book, *Shotgunning: The Art and the Science*, nearly thirty years ago. Not only did Brister frequently cite his work, but he also included a photo of a pattern developed by Roster, a handload buffered with flour, that was awfully close to 100 percent at forty yards. Yikes, it was impressive.

He is frighteningly straightforward and obviously does not suffer fools gladly. Part of this is because he really does do a huge amount of scientific research, both at the patterning boards and test shooting in the field, to examine how well average humans shoot. His manuals on reloading and barrel work are available directly from him at the following: Tom Roster, 1190 Lynnewood Boulevard, Klamath Falls, OR 97601; or call 541-884-2974 or e-mail tomroster@charter.net. Feel free to contact him; he enjoys talking with shotgunners.

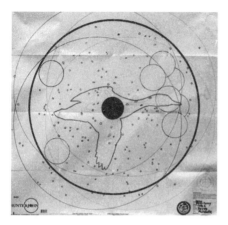

Even with all these gaps, this is a very dead duck with many pellets in the aiming circle. If point of aim is correct, then patterning targets from Hunter John are handy; if not get 48-inch wide rolls and create a 30-inch circle surrounding the densest distribution. This will also show center of impact, i.e., whether your gun shoots high or low and divergence of barrels from your point of aim. Remember that the duck is flying through the shot string.
Photo courtesy of Suzan Bruner

The following information is taken from a long telephone interview I had with Tom, which is not presented within quotation marks because I'm not sure that my scribbled notes were absolutely verbatim.

Most of what you read about shotgunning is totally unscientific. It is little more than the opinion of others, which the authors repeat but seldom test. Much of it is folk tale. If you repeat a lie or an oft-espoused theory long enough, people will come to believe it as proven fact. Unfortunately, at best, unproven theories and untested beliefs are pseudo science. For example, the truth is that no one as yet has ever found an accurate way to measure how many foot-pounds of energy it takes to kill a bird, and the exact foot-pounds have never been determined nor proven scientifically in peer-reviewed literature.

Additionally, all current downrange energy charts are based on projected values, which in turn are based on assumptions that are generally not completely valid. All such tables assume pellets are perfectly round and uniform in diameter. In reality, lead pellets are far from perfectly round; not even close. Also, lead pellets for a given size designation vary tremendously from pellet to pellet in actual diameter and actual shape. They become even more unlike one another in size and shape after undergoing deformation before they exit the muzzle. Therefore, it is an exercise in inaccuracy to try to build tables projecting their actual downrange energy and velocity.

Lead pellets also vary between lots, and within lots, and are allowed to do so under manufacturers' standards. So you can't be sure about the size or the weight of a pellet marked, say, No. 6. Even assuming you have the muzzle velocity correct, unlike dealing with a rifle bullet, you can't be certain about what is happening with velocity or energy at a given range due to those factors.

As no one has come up with an accurate way of determining how many foot-pounds of energy are required to kill a given species of bird, and because where a pellet strikes the bird and the angle at which it strikes the bird greatly affects the amount of penetration and the amount of energy that is required to kill it, it is a hollow exercise to try to absolutely quantify such a value.

At this point I mentioned to Tom that a number of writers believed that for driven shooting something on the order of 0.85 to 1 foot-pound of energy was sufficient if the bird were hit by five or six pellets. My own studies based on seeing many birds shot, and shooting something in the neighborhood of 50,000 pheasants to my own gun, has led me to the conclusion that something over two foot-pounds of energy is necessary to reach the vital organs, even on a driven bird shot from below.

Tom stated that one foot-pound of energy equals just about zilch in terms of its ability to penetrate through a pheasant and reach the vital organs on crossing or overhead shots, and especially on going-away shots.

Then he brought up another very interesting point. It takes significantly more energy to kill a bird than it does to bring it down. Wings, because they are hollow and under load, break easily. To kill requires much more energy to penetrate through skin, fat, muscle, cartilage, and even bone to reach vital organs,

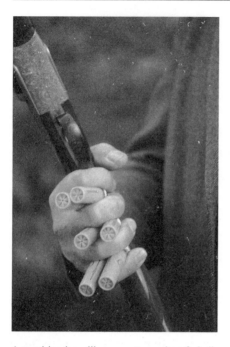

A good loader will carry extra pairs of shells in this manner, often with another pair in his teeth, crimp end first.

plus a sufficient pattern density. Tom has found and conclusively proven, via the X-ray and necropsy of thousands of waterfowl, pheasant, and turkey carcasses, that one or two pellets must intercept a lethal area with enough retained energy to puncture through to the organs in order to produce what he classifies as a "Behavior 1 Bird," one that is dead or immobile within thirty seconds.

Roster pointed out that the most important aspect that has a practical limit on the size of the load to be shot is the amount of recoil that an individual can handle. Obviously a fixed-breech gun creates more (perceived) recoil than an autoloader, and a 7½-pound gun can handle a significantly larger charge than a super light 6-pound, 12-gauge shotgun. Limits of range are in one sense determined by technology—pellet roundness, hardness, uniformity and weight, choke design, size and velocity of the payload, etc.—but are limited in another sense by the amount of acceptable recoil. The final aspect of the equation is how well the individual shoots.

According to scientific studies conducted for the Cooperative North American Shotgunning Education Program (CONSEP), which is financially supported in the U.S.A. by state and federal wildlife agencies and Winchester and Remington, and internationally by such prestigious hunting organizations as the British Association for Shooting and Conservation (BASC), the Danish Hunters Association, and the Sporting Shooters Association of Australia, Roster has found, for example, that 1¼ ounces of steel No. BBB (.190-inch) pellets from a well-patterning gun reliably kills Canada, snow, and white-fronted geese out to sixty-five yards 95 percent of the time if the shot is accurate and a minimum pattern count of fifty to fifty-five pellets for large geese and sixty to sixty-five pellets for medium-sized geese can be obtained in the thirty-inch circle at those distances.

Interested wingshooters can obtain a reprint of Roster's scientifically proven lethality table for taking gamebirds by contacting him directly. There is a small charge for the table and a reprint of the two-part article he published in *Sporting Clays* magazine explaining how the table was derived and how to use it.

Now here comes the really interesting part: Steel patterns better than lead at long range, so it actually has the potential to kill better than lead provided the proper size of steel pellet is employed. In general, a steel pellet the same size as a lead pellet won't accomplish the same job. It must be larger.

While it's possible to hand cast lead buckshot so that it is nice and round, neither the Bliemeister nor the tower-dropping method of casting will produce pellets anything close to round in sizes larger than No. 6. (You can test this by rolling the pellets on a glass plate.)

Because of the required use of nontoxic shot for much bird hunting worldwide, lead shot manufacturers today are less concerned with bird shot bigger than No. 6 (No. 5 U.K.) and are producing considerably less lead shot in sizes larger than No. 7½ than they once did. Good-quality large lead pellets, say, No. 4 and up, were possible to find twenty years ago—but no more. Because of the hardness and roundness of steel, assuming you go up to larger pellets to have sufficient weight, it will outshoot lead in the real world on waterfowl.

Hevi-Shot will kill even farther out due to its higher density and superior patterning capability, even when compared to steel shot. The problem is that most shooters must learn to point their shotguns more accurately to adjust for the tighter shot-stringing characteristics of non-deformable projectile types such as steel and Hevi-Shot. Therefore, while these projectile types possess greater killing potential than deformable projectile types like lead, the shooting skills of the average wingshooter are not strong enough to take full advantage of these potentially better performing technologies.

If lead were really well made and produced something close to the claims, or actually performed as depicted in the down-range tables, it would be pretty nifty. Unfortunately, lead craps out sooner than more modern projectile types.

In the final analysis for today's wingshooter, non-deformable projectiles such as Federal Cartridge's tungsten/iron shot or Environ-Metal's Hevi-Shot have the longest range of killing capability and will turn in the maximum performance of any cur-

Putting out dekes in a bay near Westhampton.

156

rently available shot type—lead included—in the hands of the gifted shooter.

It pays to remember that lead shot is a seventeenth-century projectile and not terribly sophisticated. The projectile's size and choke are dependent on each other. Unfortunately, manufacturers are still making chokes and regulating them to lead pellets; nobody is truly trying to design a modern choke with steel or Hevi-Shot in mind. This is a huge handicap to the potential of these projectiles. (By the way, I, Alex Brant, still love lead, especially with a high, but appropriate to the shot size, antimony level. This is a lethal and cost efficient combination. I'm certainly not suggesting that shooters categorically replace lead with tungsten, steel, etc. Rather, I just want to show the relative merits of various nontoxic shot. Never use a specific load like steel in guns or barrels for which it isn't approved, proofed, or designed.)

There are ten nontoxic pellet types on the market today. All the tungsten based loads are quite expensive and always will be. Hevi-Shot, which is a tungsten/nickel/iron combination, is undoubtedly the best. Federal's tungsten/iron loads are also outstanding, but limited in pellet size availability and payload weight. Kent makes a good tungsten/plastic combination, but it doesn't pattern quite as well as Hevi-Shot or Federal's tungsten/iron. Some of the other tungsten/plastic combinations are too soft and don't pattern well.

Incidentally, Federal's tungsten/iron loads could be very good, but they suffer from a lack of pellets in the pattern due to a super-duper wad that is perhaps the thickest wad ever made featuring double petals. The idea is that this wad will prevent the shot from ever damaging the barrels; the unfortunate corollary is that there is very little room left over for the pellets. The specific pellet has great potential, but it is limited by its delivery system and the pellets themselves are not available for handloading.

Sixty-five yards is generally considered the outer limit of shotgunning, although this could someday be greatly superseded. It may be possible to add another twenty or thirty yards if the right combination of barrel, bore size, choke, and wad were specifically designed around the various tungsten combinations. The constraints that prevent extreme shooting are not just technical. The average shooter is aging and older shooters may have trouble handling a heavy gun. The heavier the gun, the less punishing the recoil from a given load. And the bigger the payload, the greater the likelihood of a sufficient number of pellets hitting the target.

According to various studies conducted by Roster, shooters tend to prefer shorter barrels and lighter guns but in fact shoot better with long barrels, especially long, light barrels. He has also found that few shooters shoot well with light guns. His other tests have shown that most pheasant shooters are most comfortable at a range of twenty to twenty-five yards. This is where they do their best shooting and this is where they prefer to take their shots.

Roster points out that to properly pattern a gun, a given choke, and a given cartridge at a specific distance you must have a 25-round sample to have 99 percent reliability or a 10-round sample for 95 percent reliability. Few shooters are willing to do this. Most never even pattern their guns.

One of the other most important reasons for patterning your gun is to know the point of impact. As Roster points out, few hunters would take a rifle to the field without sighting it in, yet few shotgunners check for point of impact. This is even true among competitive target shooters. He has done studies on tens of thousands of people—how they shoot, how well they shoot.

The unfortunate truth is that the vast majority have never shot a clay target in their entire lives.

Shooting a few gamebirds each season won't make you a good shot. You must pattern your gun with a variety of loads and brands to find the best ones for your gun, and then practice consistently and correctly to really improve your shooting.

SQUARE LOADS

Many English writers and American Anglophiles consider the so-called "square load" the ideal. In a square load, the height and width of the pellets are roughly equal. Frankly, all I care about is the efficiency of the given load—the number of pellets and the distribution on the target.

Here's what Roster has to say on the subject: "The square load paradigm may have some validity with deformable shot types such as lead or bismuth. However, it is untrue with non-deformable shot types such as steel, tungsten/iron, or Hevi-Shot. The square load with deformable shot types allows greater room for improved shot protection, which allows such loads to pattern efficiently. Adding more pellets to a square load of a deformable shot type requires removal of pellet protection to provide room for the extra pellets, resulting in more shot deformation. This in turn results in lower pattern efficiency. With non-deformable shot types, protection of the pellets against deformation is no longer the issue. The issue becomes protection of the barrel from the hard, non-deformable shot types. Therefore, if you can fit more than a square load of non-deformable shot types into a shotshell and still properly protect the barrel, the square load becomes meaningless.

"In my tests, I have found ¾-ounce, 28-gauge lead loads effective on pheasants in No. 6 (.110 inch) out to twenty-five yards, but not in .410. In .410, I have found a minimum of a ⅗-ounce lead load is necessary in No. 6 lead for pheasants out to twenty yards. The issue is shot protection again. The .410 just doesn't provide enough room for adequate shot protection of soft pellets like lead, resulting in decreased range because of the greater percentage of deformed pellets emerging from the muzzle." Roster is referring to walked-up birds. Where the bird is presenting its head/chest to the shooter as a driven bird, range for clean kills should, theoretically, increase.

Chapter

10

HOW TO HIT TALL DRIVEN GAME AND LONG BIRDS

For the last forty years I have shot at every possible chance. For the last thirty years I have shot at least a dozen serious days of driven birds annually. And for the last ten seasons I have been out on sixty to eighty driven days per season; half the time shooting, half the time running the day, and sometimes doing both. During this time I have observed all manner of shots and all types of shooters, and while everyone these days invariably claims to enjoy tall (high) birds, very few can consistently hit them. Those who do have seen the sight picture, which along with barrel speed, is the key to consistency.

First you must understand the mechanics, dynamics, techniques, and equipment or you will only imprint and perfect your mistakes. Practice does make perfect, but only if you are practicing correctly. Otherwise, you are practicing missing. If you're having a bad day always return to the fundamentals.

A very good bird at Castle Howard in Ireland, one of the two best shoots in the country.

By the way, although the following information centers around driven birds, it applies equally well to any shooting situation where high, overhead shots are a possibility, such as pass shooting doves or ducks. One reason that a driven pheasant or partridge can be killed cleanly at longish range is that it is presenting its most vulnerable areas to the shooter. (Consistently target birds in the front third to hit the head, spinal cord, or heart and lungs.) Conversely, a "walked up" bird taken from behind is much harder to kill because you must penetrate inches of skin, muscle, bone, and viscera to reach the vitals. This reduces the effective killing range for birds taken from behind.

LEAD

Let's start by discussing the differences between a tall or long bird and an average bird and between a pheasant and a clay and how this affects forward allowance. Today's fashion on driven shoots is to shoot tall birds. (For most guns, unfortunately, it is *only* to shoot at tall birds.) It is the ultimate shooting sport. I define a tall bird as being between forty yards high and the limit of shot penetration, prior to pattern dissipation.

The difference between a clay at fifty yards and a pheasant at fifty yards is that, unless sloped downhill to work with gravity, a clay's speed is continuously and rapidly diminishing from the moment it leaves the trap arm. A pheasant, on the other hand, is maintaining or increasing speed. The line, too, plays a big part but let's not get ahead of ourselves.

Lead is a function of distance, angle, and speed. The easiest way to get a feel for this is at a clay course. Set up a straightforward forty- to fifty-yard crosser, without curve or optical illusion. Use a soft or medium spring and a 110mm

This is not what I consider a sporting pheasant although the "compression factor" of a telephoto lens makes it seem a bit lower than it actually is. While the per-bird price is low in Eastern Europe, expert guidance is needed to shoot the best estates and drives.

target. Experiment until you zero in. We all perceive lead differently, and whether you shoot sustained/maintained lead, pull away, or swing through/instinctive will affect this perception.

Now set the same flight path but with a faster spring and a 90mm midi. To break the target you will probably need three or four times as much lead. Not only will you need more lead, but also more follow through or finish. I have generally found that birds need a little bit of lead, a lot of lead, or a tremendous amount of lead, depending on angle, speed, and distance. Angle changes *perceived* lead, wind affects speed and curl. Tall pheasants need between a lot and a tremendous amount of

Dr. Jon Liland ran really first-rate and deluxe shoots in Denmark in the early eighties. He is an excellent shot with his own style. With a few exceptions, most estates and most drives in Denmark show pheasants that today would be considered mediocre.

forward allowance. Remember always: Gun movement (barrel speed) kills birds.

This big lead, coupled with finish, brings down tall birds, assuming the following: (1) you are on the right line; and (2) you use large enough shot and sufficient choke.

Let's look at how a pheasant flies. Because of its large body size relative to its small heart and chest muscles, the bird is only able to flap its wings for about seven or eight seconds. Then, like a sprinter that has given his all, it runs out of steam and cannot really fly significantly for about an hour.

When the pheasant gets up, typically its first reaction is to fly to its home wood. Knowing instinctively that it cannot fly all the way home on full throttle, it attempts to gain enough altitude to glide for most of the trip. When these areas are sufficiently separate the pheasant gains great height, even over moderate terrain. (Undulating terrain improves shooting.) After the initial wing flapping establishes height, the bird then uses the remaining flapping time to adjust its trajectory or to alter its line. (It will shy from a flagman, a bright sun, an overly shiny face, the glint of a gun, etc.)

The main point is that the pheasant is often not flying on a consistent, straight line but rather on a curve, the effect of which is increased by wind to produce a curling, or most deceptively, a slipping bird. Couple those factors with a bird whose wings are set, which means that it is dipping due to gravity, and you have a very challenging target.

The old school of thought was to read the line and swing through from tail to head. You should be reaching the head as the gun reaches your face and then fire immediately. (This is a slight oversimplification, but you get the idea.) Avoid too much "cheek time" or you will tend to slow the gun, look at the bead, and miss.

This theory, similar to swing through but with less time on the face, is very good at making a novice or poor shot quickly mediocre (a step up). This type of shooter will usually kill birds consistently at a maximum range of roughly twenty-five yards depending on the individual's coordination and barrel speed.

Observing teams on my own commercial shoots for the past few seasons, I have realized that some individuals become very proficient at twenty to twenty-five yards but consistently hit the pheasant in the back third of its body when the bird is five yards higher up, and they often miss completely after another five yards or so. The reason? They haven't grasped the concept that the sight picture changes with distance.

Let's now look at maintained/sustained lead. This is the way I shoot 97 percent of my clay targets. In this method of shooting, which is very hand-eye oriented, the better exponents can break many targets with an unmounted gun. Basically you insert the barrels with the correct lead established during the mounting process (the move-mount-shoot advocated by champion shooter John Bidwell). You can fire as the gun hits your cheek, or if less

Classic partridge drives out of Spanish olive groves tend to show low to medium birds, although the occasional perdiz sits on its tail and heads towards the heavens. The loader is a little sloppy, watching the shot. To be really quick, he should be in a better position to switch guns.

confident stay with it for a moment to confirm the correctness of the sight picture. Remember to always focus on the target.

Unfortunately, I find this method impossible for reading the correct line on a curling, dropping, driven pheasant. My method is this: Prior to mounting the gun on a really tall overhead bird I shift my weight to my back foot, which gives me the most freedom of movement (this preference may in some ways compensate for my very bad back). I focus my eyes on the pheasant's head, ignoring its body, and I mount on the head. As with the pull-away method, I travel for a distance with the bird to establish the correct line. I then pull away from the bird and continue with the "found" lead for a moment to make sure I like the sight picture. When I'm happy with the sight picture, barrel speed has been established during my mounting process. I then flip my right wrist to force a good follow through. This is actually all accomplished as one movement, but I have broken it down to its components for clarity of explanation.

Some shooters may find "tucking in" at the tail and staying with that before pulling away more to their liking. On a really tall bird, I want to shoot it when it's closest, almost directly overhead but just in front of vertical. In this instance, my weight is firmly on my rear foot and my front heel is off the ground, permitting the maximum rearward bend necessary for a second shot, which is sometimes required.

While waiting for the bird, I hold my face perpendicular to the plane of the barrels and keep it still during the mounting process. The gun must be glued to your face, with your eyes locked over the barrels. I had a slump a couple of years ago. When my loader mentioned that I was moving my gun across my face, the slump ended instantly.

On a medium bird, say twenty-five to thirty-five yards up, I prefer to take it as early as possible, way in front. This allows me more time for a second shot if necessary, more time to shoot a second bird, and more time to reload. In this case my weight is on my front foot.

Some birds are best taken as crossers. In this case, you should turn your feet if there is time. Otherwise, weight your leading foot and pivot on the rear for a bird to your left. Dropping your right shoulder (for the right-handed shooter) will also make it easier to stay on a bird crossing to the left. As you pick up the bird make certain that your gun barrels are perpendicular to its path.

Now some subtleties related to line: The first thing

The shooter—running out of swing because of bad footwork—is "rainbowing" and coming off the correct line. The shot could have been salvaged if he had pivoted on his right toe and dropped his right shoulder.

to remember is that a small discrepancy at the barrel can translate to a few feet at forty yards. I once had a lovely little Italian side-by-side with which I consistently killed birds, but I too often missed straight-forward crossers with it, even though I was convinced that my lead was correct. One day I killed a crossing duck a few feet below the bird at which I was shooting. A light bulb went on: The bead was very high and I had been placing the birds above the bead, which had been sending the shot strings low. Although I later replaced the bead, I corrected on the spot by aligning the rib, not the bead, with the birds. This again addresses the importance and subtlety of sight picture and point of impact, even with a gun that does fit.

I mentioned it earlier, but the best advice I ever received for shooting driven birds came from Sir Joe Nickerson, who suggested that you pretend the crossing bird is wearing a top hat, and then shoot for the top of the hat because it is all too easy to come off the line on a crosser and shoot low.

A good coach for driven shooting is worth his weight in gold. He will make you stylish and help you achieve correct foot position and a consistent gun mount. No one can shoot well, or indeed even be correctly fitted, without a consistent gun mount.

LOADS AND CHOKES

I have just come back from the best partridge shoot I've ever experienced in thirty-five years of visiting Spain. The shoot is called La Cuesta and provides supremely tall birds. Our team had deepish pockets and was happy with overage, so they pulled out all stops and put thousands of birds over us on each and every drive. I've seen birds of this quality before, but never of this quality and quantity. And I've never seen partridge anywhere near as tall.

The lowest birds were thirty to thirty-five yards up, the majority were over thirty-five yards up, and there were plenty of birds at fifty yards, sixty yards, and even higher to challenge the best shots in the world.

This is all prelude to the best choice of chokes and loads for gamebirds taken at long range. If you shoot tall bird shoots, with the majority of birds between thirty-five and forty-five yards up, modified (half) choke really comes into its own. As I've mentioned before, all guns shoot better with a particular load. Even distribution of pellets is, perhaps, even more important than the total percentage. A pattern with holes just doesn't cut it for long-range work.

You must go to the patterning board and experiment. I rarely count all the pellets in a circle. I just do it once for a particular load and choke. This is just as accurate as doing it three times or even five times. The sample number is too low for statistical purposes anyway. One random shot gives me a decent rough guide. However, I do fire a few more shots to look for holes a bird could fly through. Numerous gaps larger than the standard clay (110mm) tell me I need to look for other loads for pheasant-sized game. Gaps larger than a midi (90mm) won't consistently hit smaller birds like dove or partridge. (You must pattern with the appropriate shot size, of course.) After I have established the two or three loads the gun seems to prefer, I get serious about patterning for long-range shooting.

On a really long pheasant, duck, or dove, you'll be pointing the shotgun, perhaps half a dozen bird lengths in front of your target, to hit it. No one swings fast enough to shoot at a bird at long range without seeing a gap.

Bob Brister, for *Shotgunning: The Art and the Science*, patterned thousands of loads to try to get to the bottom of what really does work. Much of the stringing that occurs in a shotgun pattern happens at the base of the load where pellets are deformed on ignition. As discussed elsewhere, this can be overcome to a certain extent through the use of extra hard lead with a high antimony count, buffered loads, and special wads. Factory loads, again using buffered shot, often provide very even and very dense patterns. Another advantage of buffering is that fewer pellets are deformed, and affected pellets are deformed less.

This translates to greater penetration at the fringes of the pattern. One reason super-high velocity loads don't work as well is that they deform more pellets at the base of the wad. And a good deal more recoil is associated with faster loads, yet there is almost no difference in terminal ballistics. For example, a No. 4 pellet launched at 1,330 fps retains 2.49 foot-pounds of energy at sixty yards. With a "non-magnum" muzzle velocity of 1,235 fps the pellet retains 2.32 foot-pounds of energy. (All of these measurements are computer generated and some assumptions as to roundness and size uniformity are incorrect. Nevertheless they are useful as a relative guide so don't take these numbers as literal or correct.)

No pheasant is going to notice the .17 difference from the magnum load. Brister concluded that a 1¼-ounce buffered load with extra hard shot is the overall best load. My "clinical" studies are in total agreement. With this load it's (theoretically) possible to consistently kill duck at sixty yards. And duck are much harder to bring down than pheasant, assuming both are shot in the chest, as duck have bigger chest muscles, more fat, and denser plumage.

In a good year I probably kill three to five thousand driven birds to my own gun. Certainly this does not make me Lord Ripon or Joe Nickerson, but I do know that if I'm shooting 1⅛-ounce loads on birds over forty yards, I will hit birds that keep on going, whereas a similarly hit bird with 1¼ ounces is much more likely to come down quickly. I also like to use a 7½- or 8-pound gun for these loads.

There is an English rule of thumb that for a shotgun to be comfortable in terms of recoil it should weigh ninety-six times the shot load. For example, a one-ounce load would match up with a six-pound gun. I've also seen this "rule of ninety-six" referred to as the "ninety-nine rule," but the former is, I believe, correct and more convenient in terms of arithmetic.

Classic partridge require different choking depending on how the individual gun

Henrique Menezes shooting super tall partridge at La Cuesta: He uses a beautiful pair of Arrizabalaga, perhaps the best Spanish gun maker.

takes them. If you shoot like a Spaniard and are trying to kill the first bird forty yards in front, then modified choke makes sense. Indeed, choking could be very much like your grouse guns. If, however, you wait until the birds are on top of you then cylinder is better. It is the tendency of shooting them late that I think has given traditional partridge shooting, most unfortunately, a bad name in the eyes of some gunners. To kill one partridge at fifteen to twenty yards is no big deal. But to shoot them the way a Spaniard does—shooting two birds way in front, then two more just in front and perhaps one of two more behind—is very sporting indeed. It is just not easy to be that quick. The best Spanish shooters are really, really fast, taking four birds in the time most gringos would shoot one or two. Classic partridge do not need much shot; one ounce or even ⅞ ounce would be sufficient. A shot size of No. 6 or 7 would be ideal depending upon how your particular gun patterns.

PATTERNING AT A DISTANCE

Schrödinger, the brilliant physicist from the early part of the last century, explained in a formulaic way while describing electrons/photons why light sometimes appears to behave as wavelengths while at other times as particulate matter (the Schrödinger wave/particle duality formula). Shotgun patterns need to be thought of in a similar, though not so rigorous, fashion.

As normally conducted, shotgun patterning looks at a three-dimensional event in a two-dimensional way. In reality, shot travels like a swarm of bees through the air. Looking at a sheet of standard patterning paper (48 by 48 inches) after the shot, there is no way to tell which pellets struck when. While some center pellets probably led the pack, a pellet dead center still might not have come from the front of the shot column. In fact, most models show the front pellets being sluffed to the sides due to the forces of air resistance against leading pellets as they exit the barrel.

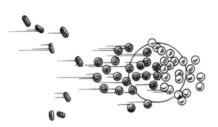

Pellets from the back of the pack become fliers due to setback forces. (Pellet deformation is exaggerated for ease of visualization.)

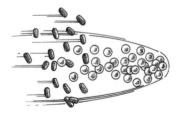

Some of the leading pellets are also pushed away by air resistance.

Shotgunning author Bob Brister's work with a fourteen-foot patterning board pulled by car clearly demonstrated the effect of shot stringing. He showed that on a fast-moving target the pellets at the front of the shot string can have a significantly different impact point than those at the back at various yardages.

We make a number of assumptions at the patterning board and on the clay field that are usually, but not always, correct. For example, if we chip a clay on the front, top, or back, we make certain assumptions about the lead. The bird that was chipped on the front was probably over-led. However, there can be other explanations albeit less likely.

Some shooters claim that full choke kills cleanly or misses completely, but what if we have a duck or pheasant flying out of the pattern? The lead is a bit behind. In this example, at twenty-five to thirty yards a bird that would be wounded with full choke is killed using improved cylinder. Yet with a slightly different lead picture for slightly different densities/diameter of pattern the bird that would have been cleanly missed or only tail-feathered is severely wounded due to the use of less choke. The same effects are also evident when shifting from something like a 12-gauge to a 28-gauge gun with the same amount of choke.

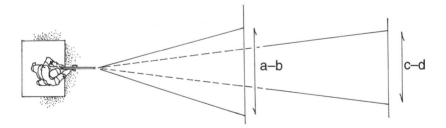

At forty yards, the useful diameter c–d is less, perhaps twenty-four to twenty-seven inches: simultaneously the degree of error to over aim is half. Both aspects make long range shooting considerably more difficult. At twenty yards, cylinder and skeet chokes give a wide margin of error a–b is about thirty to thirty-two inches. A one-degree aiming error equals about twenty-five inches at forty yards.

At this tower release in Florida, pheasants of a very high quality—even by British standards—are shown.

As the gauge diminishes, not only is this seen as diminished density within the circle, but more importantly *in terms of the width of the pattern core* and its density.

Long-distance shooting, and by this I mean shots over forty yards, is much more difficult than shooting at moderate range. Let's look at the geometry of the situation. Wide-open chokes produce a pattern with a great deal of margin of error in the fifteen- to twenty-five-yard range. This is the distance at which skeet targets or woodcock in the woods are most easily and effectively shot. Double the distance to forty yards—long, but not extreme—and the dense, effective pattern is much less forgiving. To make the equation a bit more straightforward, let's assume that we have a thirty-inch pattern at twenty yards and a twenty-five-inch pattern at forty yards.

An error of one degree translates to twenty-five inches at forty yards. That means you can be half a degree (12½ inches) above or below target, but that's all. At twenty yards, with a wider effective spread, you can be more than a degree off and still break a target or kill your bird. Had the pattern stayed at thirty inches, the margin of error would have been halved— but that is not the real world.

Let's further assume that the effective pattern is reduced with very tight chokes to fifty or sixty yards, but that the core is still intact. At sixty yards the spread, depending on the various factory loads tested with 12-bore and full choke, gave me a sufficiently dense core to humanely kill birds of ten to sixteen inches, although some loads were unacceptable performers at this extreme yardage. Tom Roster's 72-percent load at

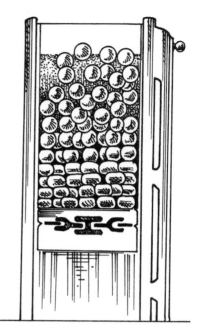

When shooting lead there will be setback deformation of pellets that cause 'fliers.' High antimony levels, buffering agents, better wads, and other factors reduce this effect. Deformation exaggerated for illustrative purposes.

sixty yards is just what the doctor ordered for this extreme shooting. At this range, a small error above, below, in front, or behind the target is much more significant. The effects are even more dramatic in smaller gauges.

REALISTIC SHOTS AT LONG RANGE

Shotgunning writer Michael Yardley once pointed out in the British magazine *The Shooting Gazette* that for many shooters twenty-five yards is the long end of killable distance. According to Rupert Godfrey in *The Shooting Gazette*, thirty-five to forty-five yards makes a good tall bird. Unfortunately, E. D. Lowry

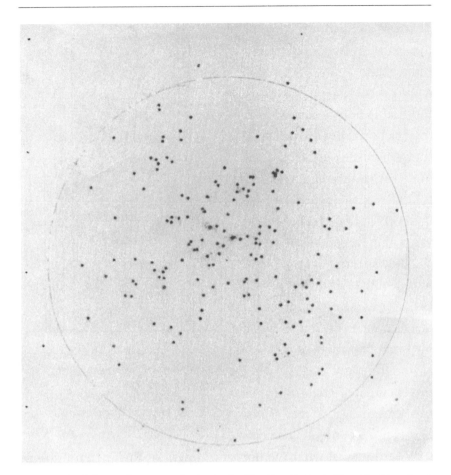

An example of the results commonly obtained with a Tom Roster buffered lead handload. This load—1¼ ounces of copper-plated No. 4s—commonly patterns above 95 percent at forty yards through a wide variety of full-choke constrictions. Here, a 99 percent pattern is produced, putting 171 pellets in the thirty-inch circle. This and other high patterning handload recipes are contained in Tom Roster's Buffered Lead & Bismuth Shotshell Reloading Manual—3rd Edition, *available on p. 151.*

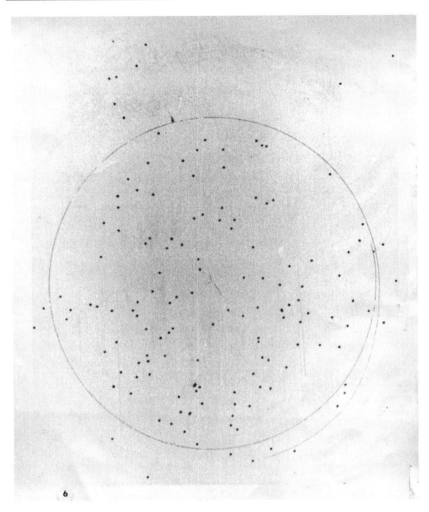

The same buffered 1¼ ounce No. 4 lead handload depicted in the previous photo is still capable of producing 72 percent efficiency at sixty yards! At this distance, fully 124 pellets still arrive in the thirty-inch circle. That's full-choke quality normally obtainable from most loads only at forty yards.

(working for Winchester/Olin) showed that even with an 80-percent pattern at forty yards a small number of birds wouldn't be humanely dispatched, both as a function of aiming errors and pattern patchiness. Yardley also pointed out, again correctly, that most shooters overestimate range. This variable can be corrected with a rangefinder. When I walk around in the country I often estimate the distance to the top of a particular tree and check this against the rangefinder to hone my skill at judging distance.

The strangest double I ever had was walking down the avenue at our place in Ireland while out doing a bit of vermin con-

COMPUTERIZED LETHALITY PREDICTIONS
PERCENT BAGGED AT AIM ERROR (DEGREES)

RANGE	(1° Aim Error is 25″ Off Center at 40 Yards)					
(YDS.)	0°	.25°	.5°	.75°	1.0°	1.25°
Modified Choke						
30	100%	100%	95%	63%	18%	3%
35	99	97	87	54	18	4
40	93	90	75	45	17	4
45	82	77	61	37	15	4
50	68	63	49	30	13	4
55	54	50	38	24	11	4
60	42	38	30	19	10	4
Full Choke						
30	100%	100%	99%	24%	1%	0%
35	100	100	90	25	2	0
40	100	100	80	25	3	0
45	100	98	68	23	3	0
50	95	86	57	20	4	0
55	82	72	46	18	4	1
60	67	58	37	15	4	1

Mallard ducks predicted to be bagged using 1½-ounce No. 4 Grex Load (Winchester Super-X Double X) used in Nilo Shotshell Efficiency Test (1972–73).

PREDICTED PERCENTAGE BAGGED—MALLARDS AT CENTER OF PATTERN

(Nilo Shotshell Efficiency Test)

Range/Yards	LOAD						
	12 Ga. Super-X 1¼ oz. + No. 4	12 Ga. Super-X 1¼ oz. No. 6	16 Ga. Super-X 1⅛ oz. No. 4	16 Ga. Super-X 1⅛ oz. No. 6	20 Ga. Super-X 1 oz. No. 4	20 Ga. Super-X 1 oz. No. 6	12 Ga. 3″ Super-X Double X Magnum 1⅞ oz. No. 4
30	100.0	100.0	100.0	99.8	99.5	99.3	100.0
35	99.2	98.8	98.9	96.8	95.1	93.4	100.0
40	94.4	92.2	93.2	86.5	83.7	79.4	99.7
45	83.9	79.0	81.8	70.6	68.3	61.9	97.6
50	69.9	62.7	67.3	53.9	53.0	45.5	91.5
55	55.7	47.3	53.1	39.4	39.9	32.4	81.6
60	43.0	34.5	40.7	28.2	29.6	22.7	69.4

trol. I shot a gray squirrel at perhaps fifteen yards, and then looked up and saw a wood pigeon at massive height. I pulled about a bus length in front of the bird with a rapidly accelerating gun. Luckily, I was shooting extra full with a 1¼-ounce load of No. 4s. The bird flew on as if he hadn't been hit and I assumed I'd missed. But then I spotted a fair clump of chest feathers at a lesser height. Looking back at the bird, now twenty-five or thirty yards on, I saw that he had stopped flapping and was stone cold dead and falling from the sky.

This occurred next to a redwood (one of the tallest trees in the country) that measured fifty-six yards high. And the bird was ten or fifteen yards higher than the tree. Over the years, I've seen pheasant, duck, and partridge killed higher than this tree on numerous occasions. At this height, partridge are the easiest to kill and ducks the most difficult. I believe this is due to the size of their breast muscles and penetration issues, despite the larger shot size used.

On some days I've killed birds at this extreme range with quite a respectable bird-to-cartridge ratio. Yet I've also had days when I struggled with thirty-yard birds due to lack of practice, a poorly fitted or borrowed gun, lack of sleep, or a bad back.

At one of my favorite tall partridge shoots in Spain the birds are driven over cliff faces a hundred yards high. They drop into range, but most are still forty to sixty yards up when they're shot. Partridge are small birds and the penetration necessary to kill them is less than for a pheasant. I've seen many cleanly dispatched in the fifty- to sixty-yard range by exceptional shots. But to a man, each gunner who shoots that well—and there aren't many—shoots a tremendous amount and shoots with guns that pattern well.

To shoot consistently at extreme range you must know yourself and your limitations. And you must know not only how well your gun patterns with a particular load, but also the point of impact for both barrels. As responsible shooters, we must all be honest about our own abilities. What one of the top shooters in the world can do at sixty yards, most of us cannot accomplish at twenty or thirty yards.

This brings us to the most important issue of all: Should you even be attempting fifty-yard shots? Birds are due the respect of being cleanly dispatched. Missing is not the worst fault in the shooting world—wounding or pricking is. If your extended range is not grounded in practice and a consistent sight picture that works, you must simply admire the bird in flight and not pull the trigger. Luck, or rather probability, shouldn't be a significant factor in the equation.

And remember: A tall, slow, straight bird is much easier to hit than a fast, close, line-altering bird. Visualize a bird traveling at sixty miles per hour. It covers the same distance over the period of, say, a second no matter whether it's five or fifty yards high. The angle, however, changes from extremely oblique to extremely acute. It is this oblique angle that makes a close bird tricky; you hardly have time to raise the gun before the bird is past. Medium birds, where you have time to focus and mount and have a relatively wide pattern, offer perhaps the easiest shot.

Chapter
11

SAFETY AND ETIQUETTE

Shotgunning is a dangerous sport. In fact, it's a very dangerous sport. The etiquette that goes with our sport is designed to minimize risk, yet we must always remain vigilant. After all, other hunters in the woods and fields might not be so careful.

I spend over a hundred days a year in the field; currently 80 to 90 percent of these days are in pursuit of birds, the rest clays. I am lucky in that at the end of a day in the office I can grab a gun and a Lab and night-flight a few ducks or walk up a few pheasants. I am often shooting with beginners or, worse, "experienced" guns that have learned to shoot on low birds. In some ways, I actually got more scared the only time that I came close to shooting someone else than when others have nearly shot me. Go figure. Strangely, even though it was not my fault, my near victim never even realized that this tragedy almost occurred.

We were shooting geese near Bahia Blanca in Argentina, one of the world's great shooting areas. Both the Magellan and the Chilean geese are fairly gullible birds; veritable cretins compared to Canada geese. They come in perhaps ten yards high and drop even lower as they approach the decoys. We were stretched out in shallow pits with camouflage netting covering us up to our chests. As we were all lying on our backs, it was fairly safe to shoot high over the feet of one's neighbor. Just as I was about to do so, the chap on my left jumped onto his knees to get a better angle at some birds behind. But by changing his position he placed himself quite close to my barrels. As I was aware of his movements in my peripheral vision, I held off slapping the trigger, or even knocking off the safety, but his stupidity shocked me.

I have a great friend in Florida with whom I shoot as often as I can. He has a great wild quail lease and a preserve license on a separate property to extend the season. He is an excellent and safe shot. However, one day another friend of his joined our small team. While this fellow shoots a fair bit, he is not what I would call a serious shooter. (And if a thought ever passed through his brain, it would die of loneliness.) We were walking in on the last covey of the day with our host on the left, Nimrod in the middle, and me on the right. As the birds burst cover plenty were going straightaway, providing safe shots for all. But Nimrod, of course, chose to lock onto a bird heading hard to the right at just about the level of my ears. All I could do was hit the deck. Truly frightening.

While the best driven pheasant shooting occurs in Great Britain, there are a few decent to good shoots in Eastern Europe. These Continental shoots work for many shooters because the bags tend to be big, the birds are at a height that doesn't discourage shooters new to driven sport, and the price is less than half the English equivalent. On one of these shoots I was invited by a friend to join a team for Hungary. Among the shooters was a megabucks guy from the dot-com boom. He brought a couple of friends with him as guests, one American who was a good safe shot and another from Holland who was a complete neophyte.

We were placed precariously close to a game crop from which the pheasants were being driven. A bird came out of the crop flying very low, perhaps at shoulder height, between me and the Dutch fellow. Obviously I did not raise my gun. But to my horror, this other fellow did, and was rapidly drawing a bead on yours truly. I yelled, "Don't shoot!" and quickly hit the ground. Luckily, he heard me in time and didn't fire. To say I was ticked off would be putting it mildly. I put down my gun, walked over, and had a quiet chat with the young man. He got the message, and to his credit I did not see him lift a gun on a dangerous bird for the remainder of the trip.

When I'm giving lessons to beginners I often shoot at the earth a few feet in front of us. The destruction is massive. Suddenly—visually and viscerally—they get the point. A mass of pellets at close range destroys all in its path. At longer range, a pellet can still blind a man. This brings us to our last example, a shoot in Denmark.

It was a well-run shoot organized by an American of Danish extraction named Dr. John Liland. Most of the team had shot driven game before and most shot quite well. There was one fellow in our group who shot a lovely pair of Purdeys. Unfortunately, once birds started to fly his blood was up—way up. A bird that he had missed in front, he decided to take behind. While you can often shoot birds behind, you must realize that they often drop behind the line; seeing sky under the bird is critical for safe shooting. This "sport" chose to shoot at a pheasant that was barely three feet off the ground. He managed to put a pellet in the dog handler's eye from quite a distance. While the eye was saved, the shooter was most appropriately asked to leave. Yet he was almost surprised.

Knowing when to shoot is not nearly as important as knowing when not to shoot. The short answer is this: If you have any doubts about the safety of the shot, don't pull the trigger—don't even mount the gun. A good rule of thumb is that any bird going directly away from you is fairly safe to target on a walked-up shoot with other gunners. This presumes that there are no houses or people in that direction. It also presumes that the bird is not so low as to endanger a dog.

If you're on the right on an upland hunt or in a blind, birds on the right are yours and birds on the left are not. That said, if your neighbor on the left is out of shells you can shoot on your left to about 45 degrees, assuming that your barrel is nowhere near your companion. It is my view that two men walking in on a point is the maximum safe number of shooters in most situations. While it's common to have three shooters in a blind, personally I'm more comfortable if there are only two.

Pointing barrels in an unsafe direction isn't the only danger; never forget that muzzle blast can permanently damage ears.

When I was twelve years old my parents sent me by train to shoot at Joe Cox's preserve. Through a misunderstanding, Joe had no idea how young I was. He was quite upset about it. At first, he wasn't going to let me shoot at all, planning instead to put me on the first train back to New York. Finally he decided to let me out on their clay field to see how I handled myself. Before we went out to the fields he said, "Do anything dangerous and I'll throw you back to New York so fast you'll beat the train." Then he went into more specific detail: "Don't point the gun at anyone or any dog, even if it's unloaded. Don't take your safety off until you're ready to shoot. Make any mistake and you're history."

I was okay on the trap field so he let me go out with a guide to shoot pheasant in the afternoon. At the end of the day his wife drove me to the train station. She was driving off and then did a U-turn. "I just had to come back and tell you that Joe said the guide told him that you were safe in the field. Joe also told me to tell you that you're welcome here as long as you continue to be safe."

While Joe often appeared to be a cantankerous old bull, he had a heart of gold. Over the years we shot together on many occasions. But unfortunately his heart of gold was weak. He went to the happy hunting grounds while I was still at college. Besides being a great shot with his Winchester Model 21, he was also a great bowhunter and even managed to kill a tiger. Fear of displeasing him instilled a great sense of caution in me, which has served me well for all these years.

Joe had a large kennel of pointers and setters, but he was particularly fond of English pointers. Normally, one or two of them would be in the house. These were great hard hunters of moderate range, but with classy running styles and 90-degree tails. From Joe I learned that only the dog handler talks to the dog during the hunt. Never give instructions to another man's dog.

Most dogs aren't trained to be steady to wing and shot, so it's imperative to know where the dog is at all times between flush and shot. If the bird is flying low, even a straight going-away shot must be ignored. Pellets spread out at a distance, and half that spread is downward. If the dog is chasing the bird it is all too easy to put pellets into the pooch. It's just not worth the chance.

Safeties are important, though not as important as having the brains to always keep the gun pointed in a safe direction. If you're the gun on the left, carrying the gun at port arms makes sense. If you're the gun on the right, don't do that. Make sure that the gun is always pointed in a safe direction, especially when closing it. I have seen guns go off when closed, even with the safety on.

It happened to me once while shooting geese on the eastern end of Long Island. Both barrels went off simultaneously, which had never happened before and never happened again with that particular gun, an old Belgian Browning. I didn't have my finger anywhere near the trigger and had just put the gun together. The safety was definitely on. My only guess as to the cause was that the firing pins were stuck down and projecting in a way that caused the discharge on closing. The only reason there was no injury was that the barrels were pointed in a safe direction.

It should go without saying, but don't take off the safety in the field until you're mounting the gun.

A few other safety concerns: When you're introducing new shooters to the sport, only load one cartridge at a time until they prove themselves safe and reasonable shots. Guns should always be broken and emptied when crossing barbwire or other obstacles. A common mistake is to remove a gun barrel-first from a vehicle. It seems too stupid to believe, but at least a few fellows have managed to kill themselves in this fashion. Always be aware of where your barrel is pointing, and where your companions are standing. If you have a moment's doubt, simply don't shoot. You may forego a few birds to the bag, but no bird that flies is worth a man's eye—or his life.

Guns are generally safe machines. The main exception to this rule is when the wall thickness of a barrel becomes too thin. This is generally not a concern with guns of recent manufacture, or American manufacture. It is, however, quite common in older, otherwise very desirable English guns. If the barrels are too thin they can be sleeved or re-lined (a new invention by Teague), or new barrels can be purchased.

It's possible to drop a 20-gauge shell in a 12-gauge barrel and to follow it up with a 12-gauge round. When this happens the barrel bursts and all hell breaks loose. Scary stuff. The simplest way to avoid this is never to carry 20-gauge shells in the same pocket, or in the same jacket, for that matter, as 12-gauge shells.

Sportsmanship is definitely an integral part of safety and etiquette. As I touched on above, if you're sharing a blind with two companions anything on the left is yours, assuming you're the gun on the left. If birds are coming directly toward you and all three gunners get up to shoot, you should start with the bird farthest to the left and work your way right.

Last October I was in a blind with my friend Tom Roulston and a guide. I was in the middle, Tom was on my left, and the guide on the right. A small group of five teal swooped around from the right and came to our decoys directly in front. We rose simultaneously. The teal kept switching position, as they so often do, but we were all up and shooting in sync. Tom killed the two on the left, the guide the bird on the right, and I took the remaining two. I don't mention this because it was brilliant shooting, although it wasn't bad, but rather because each man shot his birds. We were gentlemanly and we were efficient. The same protocol serves shooters well on a covey rise.

A couple of months before this outing I was duck shooting in Argentina. My companions were good and safe shots, but whenever a group of ducks came in there was no orderliness to the shooting. Even if there were twenty-five ducks in the air, the same duck was often shot twice. Sometimes, just as I was going to pull on my bird, someone else shot it. We were shooting a lot of birds, and I didn't know the men I was with well enough to discuss this with them or complain. Nevertheless, it did remove some pleasure from the shooting.

THE EYES HAVE IT

An old-time comedian once said, "I've been rich and I've been poor, and rich is better." To paraphrase, I've had perfect vision and I've needed glasses, and perfect vision is better.

Until I was fourteen or fifteen my eyesight was 20/20, but for some unknown reason it started to deteriorate soon after. By the time I hit college, I needed moderate lenses for accurate distant vision. I tried wearing contacts but I was never really comfortable with them. For most things it was merely a nuisance, but in sports where glasses tended to fog up it was a nightmare.

In 1998 I had laser surgery done on my eyes by one of the masters of the procedure in King of Prussia, Pennsylvania. Since then, my vision has been 20/15. I'm a very happy camper. The procedure was basically painless, but not without risk, so I'm not recommending it to anyone. However, this has given me the opportunity to experience shooting with prescription and nonprescription glasses.

A concern to all shooters is eye dominance. Most, but not all, right-handed people have a right master eye. For those new to shooting, I would actually suggest that the dominant eye determine which shoulder you shoot from. Depth perception and peripheral vision are significantly enhanced when you shoot with both eyes open. If you've already been shooting for a long time,

Eyes stay on the target while gun/upper body moves in relation to the target. (After initial D.Lee Braun—exaggerated for clarity). Photo courtesy of Renata Coleman

have master eye problems, and are uncomfortable switching shoulders, I suggest putting a piece of opaque tape on your shooting glasses over the offending eye so that it can't see the front of the barrels or the bead. (Vaseline also works.) Peripheral vision is saved but depth perception does change and you will "see lead" slightly differently.

Although my right eye is strongly dominant, on springing teal my left eye tends to see the target first and take over. I deal with this more or less successfully by squinting my left eye or by carrying an extra set of glasses with a bit of Scotch tape or a magnetized plastic disk to obscure the barrels. Attachments also can be added to the barrels to prevent the wrong eye from seeing the bead, but this is most common among the trap fraternity.

These days I tend to shoot with a number of different glasses. For competition or serious clay shooting I find that glasses from Ranger/RandolphUSA offer the greatest selection of lenses and comfort for my needs. When I just want to take one pair of glasses without extra lenses for clay shooting, I use Avian glasses from Orvis. For game shooting, I have a pair of wraparound glasses from the Bollé/Serengeti line. Optically they seem very good, although this is purely subjective, and they are the most comfortable and lightest glasses imaginable. Since I typically shoot game with other gunners nearby, I feel slightly safer with wraparounds because they protect the eye from some side angles.

When I needed prescription glasses, the work was done by Decot Hy-Wyd Company, one of the indus-

Wraparound glasses offer some protection from the side. Bolle glasses photo courtesy of Bushnell Performance Optics

The modern eyeglasses for shooters. Courtesy of Ranger/Randolph

try leaders and pioneers in glasses designed with shooters in mind.

Glass has always been the model in terms of color and the ability to see clearly (refractive index). I have an ancient pair of yellow prescription lenses, hardened for safety's sake, which I used for shooting in an equally ancient pair of Ray-Bans. They were extremely heavy, and as far as I can tell, no one uses glass in shooting glasses anymore.

CR39 is a popular lens material these days. It is a plastic resin lens that is fairly comparable to crown glass in terms of refractive index. Polycarbonate has greater impact resistance than CR39, but it isn't as good optically. I have been told—but I don't want to try it—that this material will stop a mass of pellets at thirty-five yards. There is more distortion and aberration than with CR39, and while some individuals don't notice a difference, most do. Also, polycarbonate is much tougher for companies to tint.

If you require prescription lenses, high index material will bend light quicker, which allows for a thinner, lighter lens. Optically, high index material falls between the previous two.

Colors are very important to the shooter. You want the orange target, for example, to be as visible as possible regardless of background or lighting conditions. This can't be accomplished with any one lens, so the sophisticated competitor normally has more than one at his disposal. Specific colors block specific wavelengths that prevent the eye from most efficiently viewing the target. Blocking these wavelengths from reaching the eye allows the eye/brain to better see those wavelengths needed for processing the target. This creates better contrast or depth perception.

"Under low-light conditions, for example, under halogen lights at night, Yellow Gold 15 both brightens and offers a more natural feel when shooting. It seems to take the harshness off bright halogen light," states Sam Cherry, president of Decot. "Red, rose, and purple are very good against the green background as it neutralizes the effect and makes orange more highly contrasted and visible. Bronze is very good in an open or brushy background. Orange tones are very good on duller days, as they possess enough yellow to brighten and enough red to provide contrast to clay targets.

"On very bright days colors like Rose 2 or Bronze 2 are very good, and polarized versions are best for the brightest occasions and especially good when combined with Bronze 2 or Target Sun Purple."

Polarization realigns glare/reflected light from non-vertical planes to vertical. Light reflecting off horizontal surfaces often causes some discomfort, forcing the eye to squint. And squinting reduces your ability to efficiently process images. Polarization helps our eyes to see more efficiently. Polarized lenses use iodine crystals that are positioned in vertical rows on a thin piece of film. This film is sandwiched between the two layers of lens material. The filter allows selected light to reach the eye, simultaneously absorbing reflected glare. Non-polarized sunglasses reduce visible light; however, they have little or no effect on re-

Certain colors work better at blocking out some backgrounds while highlighting the clay. Courtesy of Ranger/Randolph

flected glare. (Polarizing lenses are useful in many, but not all, shooting situations.)

If you wear prescription lenses, it is important to realize that there is a geometric center to a lens and an optical center, where the prescription is finest and most accurate. The pupillary distance is the distance between the eyes, and this must always be taken into consideration for any set of prescription glasses. Shooting glasses sit high in comparison to normal dress glasses, and the optical center must be moved higher still to allow for the natural head tilt when shooting. (In an ideal world your face would be perpendicular to the line of the ribs/barrels, but in the real world this is rarely the case.) Also, the narrow bridge common with shooting glasses raises the optical center above the midline, and by having the optical center higher it is close to the point of focus, which allows the eye to focus with greater acuity and depth of field.

If you have to turn your head this much to get your right eye over the barrels, you will wind up with a distorted view and a tight neck. Photo courtesy of Renata Coleman

Different lens shades enhance the orange target and neutralize background foliage. A particular lens shade can help the shooter concentrate on the target. Each of us perceives colors in his own fashion. Decot uses a blend of chemicals that produced their most popular lens shade ever, V-Lite Rose. The advantages of the V-Lite Rose and similar lens from Ranger, NYX, and other leading manufacturers is that they deaden the green background of foliage, highlight the orange target, and dampen the sky. Solid black targets are seen more easily by fading the background.

An aspect of gunfitting is based on getting the shooter's eye directly over the center of the rib and as perpendicular as possible. Turning your face to force the master eye into the correct position actually creates an imperfect perception of the target because depth perception is inaccurate.

The following information from Decot's web site (used with permission) explains this phenomenon: "Try looking at a small star some night: Stare at it for a moment, then slowly turn your head, at the same time keeping focus on the star. As soon as you turn your head too much you'll see the star 'double,' which means that both eyes are seeing the star individually, not as a team. If you turn your head even more you'll find that the star gets dimmer, and may even disappear entirely. What does this all mean? It's obvious! To see the best we possibly can, we should be looking straight ahead, and our heads shouldn't be tilted, either. In the back of the eye we have the retina, the screen of the eye. Light comes into the eye, strikes the retina, and is transmitted to the brain by the optic nerve. There is only one small spot on that retina where we focus perfectly."

HEARING PROTECTION

About twenty-five years ago I started a number of magazines for a company called Harris Publications. These magazines were all about shooting and hunting and included such titles as *Combat Handguns*. I was the founding editor. In this context and capacity I attended the SHOT Show, the shooting industry trade show, which was in its relative infancy. Big names still reigned in the shooting world, with Jim Carmichael, John Wootters, and a pistolero named Bill Jordan at the forefront. At a big lunch sponsored by Winchester my table included Jordan and actor Slim Pickens, who was perhaps best known as the pilot in the *Doctor Strangelove* movie who rode the H-bomb to the ground whooping and hollering all the way.

Jordan and Pickens were competing to see who could tell the best story. They were both so funny that everyone was a winner. That was the good news. The bad news was that the conversation was often a shouting contest since they had shot for many years without serious hearing protection. Indeed, for their generation, and to a lesser extent for my own, hearing protection was at best rudimentary.

As a child on the skeet range, a bit of cotton was all that was available. Soon I discovered ear valves, soft rubber things with a metal insert. They were a vast improvement over cotton. Muffs were available for use at the rifle range, but were heavy and clumsy and too large for shotgunning.

Today's shooter is spoiled for choice. But first let's discuss briefly why ear protection is so vital.

Sensor neural hearing loss is damage to the inner ear and is usually irreversible even by surgery. The main cause is deterioration of "hair" cells due to extremely loud noise. When a blast from a shotgun is sent into an unprotected ear, these delicate hair cells that transmit sound to the auditory nerve are damaged. Gunshots, the noise and waves, cause hearing loss. Loud, explosive noises are the most damaging to hearing. It is generally thought that noise in excess of 90 decibels is harmful to hearing if experienced over time. The louder the sound, the shorter the prolonged exposure needs to be to cause damage. Gunfire often exceeds 130 decibels.

Ear protection prevents damage to hearing. It's as simple as that, so wear something. Basic foam plugs provide a fair amount of protection for minimal cost. For a few bucks, simple non-electronic muffs provide lots of protection. Serious shooters often use amplified muffs or "electronic" plugs. The claim with these devices is that sound waves are limited to a safe level by miniaturized circuitry. Sounds under 80 to 90 decibels, such as speech, are actually amplified. To protect your hearing these electronic devices shut down quickly when high noise levels are perceived, but also recover just as quickly once the noise drops to a safe level.

Amplification increases your ability to hear accurately at distance. High-tech models provide an adjustable range to increase hearing up to eight times above normal with programmable units. Using current technology, it's possible to hear a pigeon coming out of a box or a clay being released from an arm while simultaneously protecting your hearing. (Actually you hear the arm; if you can hear the clay, sign up for superhero status.) And because each cup features its own electronics, they provide stereo for directional sound detection, which is very helpful to shooting flyers (boxed birds).

Some hearing protectors are custom fitted to your ear, but these require custom molds. They are comfortable but expensive, and they require fitting.

SPECIALIZED ETIQUETTE FOR DRIVEN SHOOTING

In my opinion, the apex of shooting sports is driven shooting, both from a perspective of history and difficulty. It is simulated, more or less well, at various tower releases in the U.S.A. As many Americans are just discovering this type of shooting, it may be helpful to discuss what is usually considered correct behavior and attire.

The heart of shooting etiquette lies in sportsmanship and fair play. By the way, proper etiquette will also make you popular in the dove field or duck blind. It isn't good form to shoot your neighbor's bird, a bird that's too low, or a bird clearly out of range that will at best be wounded. You should also be on time, have a gift for your host (unless you're a paying gun), and cash-tip loaders and keepers, generally twenty quid ($35) for the first hundred birds, a tenner ($18) for each additional hundred.

You should have a ready gun in sleeve, cartridge bag filled, and raingear on, if necessary, all completed early enough not to cause delay in departure. When "pegs" are drawn, unless stated otherwise, assume that with each drive you go up two numbers (i.e., in a line of eight, six becomes eight, seven becomes one, eight becomes two, and so on). Ground game should never be shot because it is too dangerous for the beaters. And I prefer the rule, "no birds behind the line," because I see too many "cowboys" in the field who feel it is more important to kill than lose a shot.

Also, many guns keep a shot-to-bird ratio. Some, preferring to keep the ratio low, choose not to cleanly dispatch a wounded bird with the second barrel, preferring to go to another bird if presented. This is inhumane and poor sportsmanship. Personally, I don't consider it poaching to dispatch a neighbor's pricked bird if he chooses not to or if his gun is empty.

A day of driven shooting is very different from a day of walk-up shooting or tower shooting. The following protocol, mostly provided in random order, should give you a feel for safety, behavior, convention, and equipment.

WHAT TO BRING

For all countries in Europe you will need gun licenses and hunting licenses, which can generally be handled easily by the agent or operator. In the U.K. you're required to have a current valid license to hunt game; this can be purchased at any post office. Without it you are deemed to be in breach of the law (poaching) and your insurance will be considered null and void. And you will need third party insurance liability, which can be purchased from Countryside Alliance or British Field Sports Society.

You'll also need the following:

- A suitable gun or guns. It is invariably a good idea to bring a spare gun or spare locks, or at minimum, springs and firing pins.

- An auto safety is preferred and should be required if you're shooting double guns. (Guns should always be closed, with the barrels pointing to the ground.)

- A gun sleeve, preferably leather and well padded to protect the gun. It should have a well-made shoulder strap. Double gun cases are very posh.

- A cartridge bag in leather or canvas/leather. Ideally, this should be a speed bag capable of carrying at least a hundred cartridges and with a wide mouth for ease of loading.

- Ear and eye protection. Too often Guns (aka shooters) on driven shoots forego one or both.

- Plenty of appropriate cartridges. Nontoxic shot is required in England for waterfowl. In the Republic of Ireland lead is legal.

- Shooting gloves and hand warmers.

- Cash for the keepers, loaders, and pub.

- A well equipped gun might choose to carry a cartridge extractor, a cleaning kit, a hand guard for a side-by-side (if you are single gunning), a hip flask (traditionally filled with Sloe Gin), cigars (preferably Habanas), and a small first-aid kit (bandages, eye drops, Neosporin, tweezers, and lip salve).

APPROPRIATE DRESS

- A warm water-resistant jacket in muted shades of green or brown. I prefer the classic Barbour waxed variety.

- Rubber boots, ideally Hunter or a copy of their style with the side zipper.

- Waterproof leggings.

- A tweed cap, not a deerstalker, which should be worn only for deer stalking unless you're Sherlock Holmes, plus a waxed cotton waterproof hat or dark tan hat made by Filson, as these are the best for keeping off the rain.

- Suitable ties and shirts; Tattersall patterns are ideal for the shirts.

- A warm comfortable pullover or cardigan sweater.

- Tweed suit (jacket and breeks need not match), with jackets designed for shooting and with breeks, or plus two, or my own favorite, plus fours. Nothing should look too new.

- Thick hand-knitted woolen shooting socks with knitted trailing garters are the one area of dress where one is allowed to be exuberant in a color sense.

Chapter

12

CLEANING UP

Answer: Your dogs, your guns, yourself.

Question: In what order do you end a day of shooting?

There are few pleasures as great as sitting in front of a roaring fire at the end of a great shoot day, heartily puffing on a Cuban cigar and sipping a single malt, telling jokes, discussing shots, embellishing prowess. But don't run too fast to the comfort of a wing chair. First things first.

If you have a gun dog you should always give him a quick once-over after a day afield. Dogs often pick up seeds in their eyes, so that is where you should start. A solution to rinse out the eyes is imperative, and optic ointment is also very handy. Next, check the paws and the pads and between the toes. Tweezers are useful for extracting thorns or stickers. Finally, check his body for cuts from barbwire or other materials. For minor cuts, you can clean the area and apply a special skin adhesive that works like Crazy Glue. Great stuff. (Never use Crazy Glue, which isn't formulated for use on skin.)

Next, look to your guns. If the day has been dry all you need to do is wipe the guns with a Silicon cloth. Unfortunately, many

This loader is getting ready for a day of shooting. Loaders in the British Isles often take their appearance more seriously than the Guns.

shooting days are spent in wet conditions. From the Outer Hebrides to Lincolnshire to upstate New York I have shot in rain that seemed to be pounding sideways. And I've been in hailstorms in supposedly sunny Spain. On such occasions a thorough cleaning is vital.

All too often, shooters wait until they get home to wipe down their guns. But rust can start during even a short car ride. This is exacerbated if the gun is in a sleeve, especially a wet sleeve. Often gents on driven shoots let their loader or the keeper clean their guns. This is great if those guys know what they're doing, but it's a disaster if they don't. Sometimes they apply oil so liberally and badly that your wood stock is doomed. Personally, I prefer to do this task myself.

I usually carry a couple of old, dry, soft, clean towels so I can wipe everything down. Be sure to get into the crevices, especially where the ribs meet the barrels. After I'm sure everything is dry, I wipe all metal again—the external metal, that is—with a Silicon cloth. Next I take a cleaning rod and push a small bit of paper towel down the barrel. I'm not trying to clean the gun for shooting at this stage, just taking a prophylactic approach to rust. Then I used a can of compressed CO_2 to blow out areas that are hard to reach,

Removable trigger groups are great because they are easy to clean after a wet day afield. Photo courtesy of Beretta

such as between the rib and the top of the barrels for guns with ventilated ribs. Q-tips and toothbrushes are very useful for getting into little nooks and crannies near the breech face. Next I spray the barrels inside and out with WD-40, which displaces moisture. I try to leave the barrels in a vertical position before the ride home so the excess liquid can run off, ideally onto newspapers or the like. WD-40 won't rot wood, although I've been told that it's bad for case colors.

If you have a trigger-plate gun such as a Perazzi it is a good idea to drop out the trigger after a wet day, spray it with WD-40, and leave it overnight on some paper towels. Wipe it down and then lightly coat it with good-quality light gun oil.

I'm also diligent about drying all areas of the trigger guard and using the Silicon cloth or oiled rag. After wiping off the excess WD-40 I either put the gun together in a dry sleeve or, better still, in its case.

If it has been a particularly wet day of shooting, as soon as I get home I run solvent and a brass brush down the barrels, re-dry with a clean towel, and re-wipe with my trusty Silicon cloth. After using solvent on the barrels I dry them and then lightly coat them with a good gun oil. Regardless of how diligent you are in trying to superficially clean your gun on a wet day, remember that water will penetrate into the lock works through the striker holes and around the plates. Once a bit of rust has taken hold the springs are much more likely to break.

Many authorities write about the dangers of excess oil. After all, if oil runs into the stock the wood will soften. And if it runs into the action it can impair the workings of locks. But if you go to one of the top gun stores or visit their stands at the game fairs you will see that the guns are actually fairly "wet," especially on the lumps. This is the way I like my guns because it prevents scoring, and the abuse of overly aggressive loaders. The pundits who suggest applying a single drop of oil with a bird's feather are probably not shooting a couple of hundred rounds in a day.

I believe the key is to not place oil where it will seep backward into the stock or the works. One easy way of doing this is to store the gun barrel-down and forearm-off after it is oiled. Another is to make sure that you don't place too much oil directly on the action, inside or out.

Grease is much preferred on hinge pins, action knuckles, and the like, as it won't seep to other areas. I highly recommend the cleaning products of Birchwood Casey and Shooter's Choice among others.

A chamber brush does a good job on plastic fouling, which could hamper extraction or ejection. This is especially important if you

This Perazzi has a trigger that will move forward and back. A long hex screw enables one to quickly change stocks. The chamber brush, cartridge extractor, fast choke tube changer, non-marring hammer, snap caps, and special pliers for changing springs are useful accessories.

use an autoloader for "high volume" wildfowling or dove and pigeon in places like Argentina or Bolivia.

Do not periodically remove your locks to lightly apply oil unless you know exactly what you're doing. If you don't, depending on how much you shoot and how often you shoot in wet conditions, your guns should go to the gunsmith regularly. Two years is probably the maximum, and if you often shoot in wet conditions, once a year, ideally as soon as the season is over to minimize potential rust. If you do choose to remove the locks yourself make sure that you have proper gunsmith turn screws. You can probably get your local gunsmith to grind a set to suit your gun. Without proper turn screws you'll likely damage the heads of the pins.

It is good to know how to take out your ejector slides and clean them when necessary. If you no longer have a manual for your shotgun, say, because it belonged to your great-grandfather, get your local gunsmith to teach you how to do this.

Finally, if you keep your guns in a metal safe make sure that it has a dehumidifying rod or a can of silica gel to remove the excess moisture from the air. It makes no sense to take wonderful care of your guns and then store them in an environment that promotes rust.

Chapter
13

HAVE GUNS, WILL TRAVEL

Times they are a changing. When I was a young lad I never gave a second thought to jumping in a cab with a shotgun in a long soft case. I would then carry it through Grand Central Station to buy my train ticket. Gun ownership, even in New York City, was pretty hassle free in those days. In the late 1960s, following the assassinations of Martin Luther King and Robert Kennedy, New York City imposed a permit system for the possession and ownership of long arms. You had to be fingerprinted and go through a lot of red tape.

Post 9/11, I must admit that I feel at least slightly awkward when traveling through Grand Central just carrying a gun in a take-down hard plastic case. I still do it, of course, and most travelers probably assume that I'm carrying some type of musical instrument.

Traveling with guns has always been fraught with some peril. Loss is always at the top of the list. The second problem is that bags are sometimes left behind by airlines. This is most common when the first leg of a connecting flight is delayed and bags don't make it over fast enough. This happened to me once on the way to Madrid; the bags didn't arrive for a number of days.

Another time I checked into Heathrow in London, thinking I had plenty of time for my flight to Dublin. My bag, once collected by security, should have made the flight, but it did not. The real problem in this instance was that the guns traveled on another flight three hours later. Aer Lingus refused to deliver them, so I had to pay the driver to return to the airport and retrieve my bags—over an hour each way. Customs and immigration couldn't have been easier, and they just gave him the guns and let him proceed. I had given him all the necessary paperwork, but they didn't even bother to look at the serial numbers. I don't know another country where this would have been so smooth.

Twenty years ago foreigners traveling to the U.K. didn't need a license for shotguns, although they did need one for rifles. In those days most customs officials just took a quick look down the barrels. Today, visitors need temporary firearm certificates.

Until 9/11, visitors to America had virtually no need for paperwork. The most that was required, at least as I understand it, was a note from a shooting grounds or an outfitter saying that you were traveling to shoot. In most instances, even that formality was overlooked. Paperwork is now required for foreigners bringing firearms into the U.S.A. I've never needed to go through it, but it is my understanding that it takes a month to six weeks.

Which brings me to my next general piece of travel advice: If at all possible, make sure that paperwork is done well in advance when traveling to any foreign destination. Foreign gunners coming to shoot ducks or pheasants with me in Ireland frequently waited until the last minute to send in their paperwork, even though they had booked their hunts months before and received forms in a timely manner. Ireland is a pretty easy place and we knew the various agencies well, but it caused a headache for all involved.

It is also important to use an appropriate hard case, plastic or metal, when traveling. I prefer metal cases because I think they make it harder for careless baggage handlers to damage guns. However, there are times when weight limitations are an issue, and outstanding molded plastic cases are also

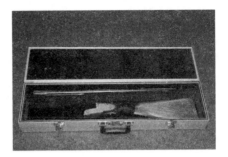

A sturdy, well-designed case will ensure that your gun will arrive intact. This Americase design is one of the best.

available. My favorite cases for carrying side-by-side or over-under shotguns come from Americase, which offers models for single and double guns. My other favorite metal case is made by a company called Kalispel. Their aluminum double gun cases easily house two large semiautomatic shotguns taken apart. (Their case can obviously be used for side-by-sides or over-unders, as well.) Where weight is a concern, I like the excellent full-length cases from Plano and Dosko Sport, which even have rollers for easy airport transfer.

With tightened security at airports, extra planning and preparation are now necessary—some airlines, low-frill Ryanair, for example, no longer accept guns. It is your responsibility to become familiar with the special regulatory requirements for transporting shotguns. Obviously, shotguns and ammunition are prohibited from carry-on luggage but can be legally transported as checked baggage, at least

Americase makes cases that even Neanderthals would have a hard time damaging. This one carries a pair of side-by-sides.

with most airlines, but only if rules are followed. Similarly, many other items are prohibited in carry-on luggage, even innocuous choke tubes, stocks, trigger groups, screwdrivers, and pliers.

The Transportation Security Administration (TSA) web site is an excellent source for general information (www.tsatraveltips.us or call 1-866-289-9673). This site also maintains an up-to-date section for "Permitted and Prohibited Items." Things change, so always check when booking and again just before traveling.

You also need to be aware of any state or local restrictions on carrying firearms. If in doubt, check with a local gun shop. Such places can usually provide good information, but you should still check it against other sources. If you're traveling internationally, your agent or outfitter can help you comply with all rules and regulations.

Each airline's rules for handling firearms differs, and some impose additional restrictions or fees. Check your airline's web site and read their rules for accepting and handling checked firearms. And recheck a day or two before the flight to make certain that the rules haven't changed. It is smart to print out these rules and bring them with you in case the agent tells you something different when checking in.

You must declare all guns and cartridges when checking in. The shotgun must be unloaded (of course), packed in a locked hard case, and be partially disassembled. For shotguns, just separate the barrels and forend from the receiver. Only you may have the key or combination to the case.

You are required to pack ammunition in a separate container from the firearm. (I generally leave cartridges at home except when traveling to South America, where shells are very expensive. I carry some shells only if excess baggage fees are not incurred.) The ammunition must be boxed in cases specifically designed to carry ammunition. Check with your airline to determine if there are any other limitations, such as weight or packaging.

Allow extra time at check-in for the declaration and inspection process. As agents may not be aware of the proper procedures, it is extremely important to remain polite and understanding. The agent will inspect the cased firearm to verify that it is unloaded and you will be required sign a Firearm Declaration Form SS-161, declaring that the firearm is unloaded. Then relock the case, and depending on the airline, either take your gun case to the screening area or hand it to the ticket agent. Regulations require that all checked baggage be screened for explosives. It is recommended that luggage be left unlocked, but this does not apply to cases containing firearms. (On one trip to Argentina my waders evidently seemed suspicious to the overzealous screeners, who went over the felt bottoms with the proverbial fine-toothed comb.) All gun cases must remain locked after the declaration process.

If a screener detects something suspect or chooses to open the gun case, they will have the airline's representatives contact you to provide the key or combination. Pay special attention to public address announcements in the airport or gate to avoid unnecessary delays. Again, try to remain polite and courteous even if dealing with thick-headed or overcautious agents. Especially if dealing with these people—they still have the ability to make things difficult for you.

Appendix

GEAR, GADGETS, AND GOODIES

I've made a few specific product recommendations here and there throughout the text, but the following is a round-up of some of the things I've found most useful during my years of shooting.

Many a day afield has been ruined by a gun that quit. Sometimes a broken firing pin/striker or spring that has given up the ghost may require a gunsmith's attention. It's a good idea to carry spare firing pins and springs from the gun maker. If you're traveling, a local gunsmith may be able to change them for you, but he likely won't have the parts you need at hand. Sometimes you may be able to get by on your own. For example, changing the springs on a Perazzi is fairly straightforward. But to do the job right you need a tool from the gun maker or a ground-down set of pliers. Changing firing pins on a Perazzi is not so simple.

I recommend that you go to your local gunsmith and have him show you a few simple things you can do yourself in the field when the need arises. Have him set up an appropriate tool kit for you. Brownells puts out a shooting supply catalog so

Modern shotguns evolved from flintock beauties like this Purdey. Shooting was much more complicated and less reliable back then. Vintage shotguns are highly sought by collectors. Photo courtesy of Purdey

big that when the new one comes out, you can use the old one for penetration tests. Here you'll find everything you need for do-it-yourself projects, from specialized screwdrivers to checkering tools to equipment for virtually any task.

I was on a driven shoot one time with a friend and his father when the latter's Boss refused to go together. After a little bit of investigation, I realized that I needed to recock the self openers of the forend. Being a germaphobe, I just happened to have a little plastic rectangular jar of antibacterial hand agent on me. I was able to save the day by using the jar to push the ejector cams forward toward the push-button end of the forend. A dowel flattened on one side is also handy for this and similar jobs.

Both Kershaw and Leatherman make wonderful multi-tools that you can wear on a belt or throw in a bag. They now come with interchangeable screw heads that are very useful. These tools can literally save an outing; carry them always. Kershaw also makes excellent knives and shears, and the latter are great for cutting off wings and so on when dressing out birds.

I have not done much reloading; indeed, it is an aspect of my education that is sorely lacking. However, after studying the work of Tom Roster I have decided to give it a whirl. To this end, I have acquired a MEC 9000 reloader with which I plan on trying to replicate his results. Of course, my work will be much eas-

Geese respond very well to motion. Photo courtesy of Wing Wavers, Inc.

ier because I already have his manuals to guide me. Tom's books on reloading and barrel work are available by writing to Tom Roster, 1190 Lynnewood Boulevard, Klamath Falls, OR 97601; or call 541-884-2974 or e-mail him at tomroster@charter.net.

Tom Roulston, my great pal, is one of the most successful duck hunters in the Midwest. This is not a matter of luck. He possesses considerable hunting skill and has access to some exceptional wetlands. He also uses motorized decoys. Put simply, they work. Motorized units from OpenZone (Flapp'n Duck, Landin' Duck, Flapp'n Goose, and Glide'n Duck) and jerk-cord-operated flapping silhouette deeks from Wing Wavers will undoubtedly increase your success.

Flapp'n Ducks add motion that really does seem to pull in wildfowl. The motion of the wings gets the attention of ducks at a distance in ways static units do not. Wing Waver decoys have become very popular as an effective "finishing" decoy. The company's owner, an avid waterfowler, became frustrated with flagging. After capturing the attention of birds, he found flagging ineffective when the birds drew nearer and the motion had to be stopped. He wanted a decoy that "could finish the job." His thirty years of waterfowling experience allowed him to invent these innovative flapping silhouette decoys. By the way, motorized units are restricted or illegal in states like California, Washington, Oregon, Pennsylvania, and Arkansas; Minnesota has a partial season ban.

When I'm hunting ducks and geese I like to keep my shells in a waterproof lightweight plastic box from Plano. I store my Quaker Boy calls in it, as well. I think these calls are excellent, and their instructional tapes are extremely useful.

My favorite muff-style hearing protectors are from a series called Pro Ears, made by RidgeLine. To protect your hearing while still being able to listen to all normal sounds you must use

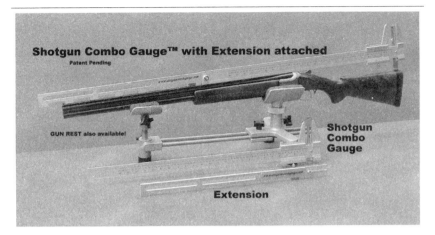

A Shotgun Combo Gauge allows the serious tinkerer to accurately take most gunfit measurements. Photo courtesy of Shotgun Combo Gauge

an electronic device that shuts down quickly when high noise levels are perceived, but also recovers just as quickly once the noise drops to a safe level. Pro Ears claims to offer the fastest "attack time" in the industry at 1.7 milliseconds.

E.A.R., Inc., makes great electronic plugs, most, but not all, of which require custom fitting. They also make outstanding shooting glasses, NYX.

For hunting in cold, wet weather the best and most convenient boots I've ever worn come from a company called Hunter. They are to British boots what Barbour is to British coats. I prefer their zip-sided models.

The Robert Louis Company makes a great gunfitting device, called the Shotgun Combo Gauge, for measuring length of pull, drop, and pitch. It is light, affordable, and accurate, and if you take stock measurements seriously it's definitely worth owning. It does not give a precise cast dimension, but you'll still get a good idea. It's also easy to use, which is always a plus. This tool is particularly helpful for resetting an adjustable trap stock.

Graco Corporation makes aftermarket adjustable-comb stocks for a number of guns, which can be very appealing for trap shooters. They also make barrel weights that can help with a gun's balance and reduce recoil.

Cole Gunsmithing offers well-figured and exhibition-grade stocks for Beretta and other makes. They do an excellent job—the checkering is fine and the finish oil is very good indeed.

For the ultimate custom barrel work—patterning, hand honing chokes for a specific load, changing point of impact—Ken Eyster's Heritage Gunsmith is *the* place to go.

Kick-eez makes a great line of recoil-absorbing pads composed of Sorbothane. This is a great material for handling recoil, which can cause some shooters to develop a very detrimental flinch.

Birchwood Casey and Shooter's Choice offer an excellent variety of cleaning products.

The one catalog I cannot live without is Orvis. They have a wide range of products and clothing for shooters.

Columbia and Woolrich produce excellent coats, vests, and pants in camouflage and normal colors for the upland gunner and waterfowler.

A long hex screwdriver like the one that comes with a Perazzi is necessary for removing your stock. Chamber brushes are often overlooked—don't make that mistake. A cartridge extractor is nice to have but less necessary than in the old days when paper hulls prevailed. Cotton gloves are useful for handling guns before storing them for a long time, as they prevent corrosive fingerprints.

My favorite booking agency for the traveling sportsman is Driven Shooting (www.drivenshooting.com). From Argentina to Spain and from Great Britain to Africa, they only associate with the best lodges and outfitters. Of course, I have to admit that I'm biased. I own it.

CONTACT INFORMATION

Aero Outdoors
316 E. B. Circle
Pasco, WA 99301
509-545-8000; 509-546-2001 (fax)
info@aerooutdoors.com

Americase
1610 E. Main Street
Waxahachie, TX 75165
1-800-972-2737; 972-937-8373 (fax)
www.americase.com

Armory Publications
2120 S. Reserve Street
PMB253
Missoula, MT 59801
www.armorypub.com

Barbour, Inc.
55 Meadowbrook Drive
Milford, NH 03055
1-800-334-3474
www.barbour.com

Beretta Gallery
718 Madison Avenue
New York, NY 10021
212-319-3235; 212-207-8219 (fax)

Beretta USA Corporation
17601 Beretta Drive
Accokeek, MD 20607
1-800-BERETTA; 301-283-0189 (fax)
www.berettausa.com

Birchwood Casey
7900 Fuller Road
Eden Prairie, MN 55344
1-800-328-6156 or 952-937-7933
www.birchwoodcasey.com

Briley
1230 Lumpkin
Houston, TX 77043
1-800-331-5718
www.briley.com

Brownells
200 South Front Street
Montezuma, IA 50171
1-800-741-0015
www.brownells.com

Bushnell Performance Optics
9200 Cody
Overland Park, KS 66214
1-800-423-3537
www.bushnell.com

Casa de Campo
Shooting Center and Resort
P.O. Box 140
La Romana, Dominican Republic
809-523-3333, ext. 5145
www.casadecampo.com.do

Cole Gunsmithing, Inc.
P.O. Box 19
21 Bog Hollow Road
Harpswell, ME 04079
1-800-650-2653; 207-833-5677 (fax)
dc@colegun.com

Columbia Sportswear
14375 N.W. Science Park Drive
Portland, OR 97229-5418
1-800-547-8066; 503-735-4593 (fax)
www.columbia.com

David & Charles Book Publishers
Brunel House, Forde Close
Newton Abbot, Devon TQ12 4PU
United Kingdom
011-01626-323254

DoskoSport
Doskocil Manufacturing Company,
    Inc.
P.O. Box 1246
Arlington, TX 76004-1246
817-467-0441; 817-472-9810 (fax)
info@doskosport.com

Driven Shooting International
    Booking Agency
Alex Brant
16 East 71st Street
Suite 2A
New York, NY 10021
212-744-9510
brant@drivenshooting.com
www.drivenshooting.com
    or
Humewood Castle
Kiltegan, County Wicklow
Ireland
011-353-5964-73215
Fax: 011-353-5964-73382
info@drivenshooting.com
www.drivenshooting.com

E.A.R., Inc.
Insta-Mold Division
P.O. Box 18888
Boulder, CO 80308
1-800-525-2690; 303-447-2637 (fax)
www.EARinc.com

Federal Premium Ammunition
Federal Cartridge Company
900 Ehlen Drive
Anoka, MN 55303
1-800-322-2342; 763-323-2506 (fax)
www.federalpremium.com

Graco Corporation
P.O. Box 940
104 Oak Drive
Gravette, AR 72736
479-787-6520
www.graco-corp.com

Higdon Decoys
230 Lake Pointe Drive
Paducah, KY 42003
270-534-8792
info@higdondecoys.com

Hunter Boots (available widely
    in the U.S.)
The Hunter Rubber Company
    Limited
Edinburgh Road
Dumfries DG1 1QA Scotland
United Kingdom
011-440-1387-269-591
Fax: 011-440-1387-250-995
www.hunterboots.com

Hunter John (patterning targets)
P.O. Box 771457
St. Louis, MO 63177
www.hunterjohn.com

James Purdey & Sons, Ltd.
57-58 South Audley Street
London W1K 2ED
United Kingdom
011-44-207499-1801
Fax: 011-44-20-7355-3297
enquires@james-purdey.co.uk

Kalispel Case Line Products
P.O. Box 267
Highway 20
Cusick, WA 99119
509-445-1121; 509-445-1082 (fax)
sales@kalispelcaseline.com

Kershaw Knives
25300 S.W. Parkway Avenue
Wilsonville, OR 97070
503-682-1966

Kick-eez, Inc.
301 Industrial Drive
Carl Junction, MO 64834
www.kickeez.net; www.kickeez.org

Krieghoff International, Inc.
P.O. Box 549
Ottisville, PA 18942
610-847-5173
www.krieghoff.com

Leatherman Tool Group, Inc.
P.O. Box 20595
Portland OR 97294
503-253-7826
mktg@leatherman.com

MEC
715 South Street
Mayville, WI 53050
920-387-4500
www.mecreloaders.com

OpenZone, Inc.
1136 Via Verde, #198
San Dimas, CA 91773
1-866-791-7575; 626-332-8979 (fax)
admin@openzone2000.com

Orvis Company
Historic Route 7A
Manchester, VT 05254
1-800-235-9763
www.orvis.com

Plano Molding Company
431 E. South Street
Plano, IL 60545-1601
1-800-874-6905; 630-552-9737 (fax)

Pro Ears
RidgeLine Products
101 Ridgeline Drive
Westcliffe, CO 81252
1-800-888-EARS
www.pro-ears.com

Quaker Boy Game Calls
5455 Webster Road
Orchard Park, NY 14127
1-800-544-1600

Ranger Shooting Systems
26 Thomas Patten Drive
Randolph, MA 02368
1-800-541-1405; 1-800-875-4200 (fax)
www.randolphusa.com

Remington Arms Company, Inc.
P.O. Box 700
870 Remington Drive
Madison, NC 27025-0700
1-800-243-9700
www.remington.com

Robert Louis Company, Inc.
31 Shepard Hill Road
Newtown, CT 06470
1-800-979-9156; 203-270-3881 (fax)
www.shotguncombogauge.com

Safari Outfitters
Route 44
Millbrook, NY 12578
www.safarioutfittersltd.com
845-677-5444

Shooter's Choice Gun Care
Ventco Industries, Inc.
15050 Berkshire Industrial Parkway
Middlefield, OH 44062
440-834-8888; 440-834-3388 (fax)
www.shooters-choice.com

Wing Wavers, Inc.
6410 Oxford Street
St. Louis Park, MN 55426
952-922-0404
info@wingwavers.com

Woolrich
2 Mill Street
Woolrich, PA 17779
1-800-966-5372
www.woolrich.com

SUGGESTED READING

The following is a short list of standard shooting references.

Braun, D. Lee *Skeet Shooting with D. Lee Braun.* Rutledge Books, 1967. (This excellent little book is the perfect primer on skeet shooting.)

Brister, Bob. *Shotgunning: The Art and the Science.* Winchester Press, 1976. (This American classic should be in every shotgunner's library.)

Fjestad, S. P. *Blue Book of Gun Values.* Blue Book Publications, 2005. (This book is updated every year, and it's an excellent source for evaluating the correct price for most firearms. I find the prices for used guns of current manufacture slightly high. Nevertheless, this is a good starting point, and excellent for older guns.)

Greener, W. W. *The Gun and its Development.* The Lyons Press, 2002. (A classic on both sides of the Atlantic.)

Hastings, MacDonald. *Robert Churchill's Game Shooting.* Countrysport Press, 1990. (This is one of the classics, and while I completely disagree with instinctive shooting for long shots or for anyone who wants to truly excel at shooting, there is a tremendous amount of useful information and easy-to-follow illustrations. My own recommended foot positions are quite similar to Churchill's—a narrow stance with the left foot slightly leading. He was a very stocky fellow with a short neck, and this no doubt affected much of his technique.)

Hoyem, George, ed. *History and Development of Small Arms Ammunition*. Armory Publications, 1999.

——*British Sporting Guns & Rifles*, Volumes 1 and 2. Armory Publications, 1996. (Both of these titles are hugely informative for the technologically inclined historian or collector.)

Milner, Robert. *Retriever Training: A Back to Basics Approach*. Ducks Unlimited, 2002. (I recommend all of Robert Milner's books on retriever training. He also has produced some excellent retriever training videos.)

Oberfell, George G., and Charles E. Thompson. *The Mysteries of Shotgun Patterns*. Oklahoma State University Press, 1957. (This is the classic treatise on pellet distribution, but it's difficult to locate a copy these days.)

Ohye, Kay. *You and the Target*. Self-published, 1978. (An extremely useful primer for trapshooting.)

Ramage, Ken. *Gun Digest*. Krause Publications, 2005. (This great reference is published annually.)

Tarrant, Bill. *Best Way to Train Your Gun Dog: The Delmar Smith Method*. David McKay Company, Inc., 1977. (A system that works and that's easy to understand and follow.)

Other useful books:

Austyn, Christopher. *Modern Sporting Guns*. Safari Press, 1994. (An excellent treatise dealing primarily with English guns and accessories.)

Bowlen, Bruce. *The Orvis Wing-Shooting Handbook.* The Lyons Press, 1985. (A good beginner's book for general game shooting with excellent sections on gunfit, although I believe it relies too much on "instinctive" shooting.)

McIntosh, Michael, and David Trevallion. *Shotgun Technicana.* Countrysport Press, 2002. (Largely derived from their columns from *The Shooting Sportsman*, but expanded nicely without the constraints of column space. This is my favorite of McIntosh's excellent series of books.)

Nobili, Marco. *Fine European Gunmakers.* Safari Press, 2002. (This is primarily a book of high-end European shotguns in current manufacture, but it also includes a fair amount on rifles. Nobili has written a number of useful reference books, mostly on Italian makers and engravers. Unfortunately, the earlier editions were so badly translated that sometimes you just had to laugh out loud.)

Petrie, Chuck, ed. *Dabblers and Divers: A Duck Hunter's Book.* Ducks Unlimited, 1996. (A wonderful photographic tribute to duck hunting.)

Reiger, George. *The Complete Book of North American Water-fowling.* The Lyons Press, 2000. (Reiger is one of the best outdoor writers, and this is an outstanding history and overview of wildfowling.)

Taylor, John. *Shotshells and Ballistics.* Safari Press, 2003. (This book has numerous attributes, but there is one underlying flaw: The author uses industry standards for pellet diameter and therefore assumes, for example, that all one-ounce, No. 6 shotshells have exactly the same number of pellets in them. Although much more time-consuming, it would have been of greater interest had each manufacturer's pellet count in a batch been tested and a computer model run. I also assume that the computer model used assumed a round lead pellet, which does not actually exist.)

Index